On the cover: Roving Blackfoot Indians were on the lookout for Shoshoni buffalo hunters who crossed to the upper Missouri to hunt buffalo, invading Crow and Blackfoot Indian territory. The fierce Blackfoot would conquer and steal their horses in Montana Territory. Hunting parties of Shoshoni learned, for their safety, to travel in great numbers to the Upper Missouri following the bison onto the Plains. The Mountain and River Crow also would give them a good fight, if discovered. Picture a long line of silent Shoshonis on horseback passing single file undetected through fierce Crow and Blackfoot country.   (Photo Courtesy of Azusa Publishing Company, L.L.C.)

D1607647

Smoke Signals &
Wagon Tracks
A history of Idaho and
the American Northwest

Robert D. Bolen

3

First Printing   2008
Second printing 2009
Third Printing   2012

Copyright 2008
Second Edition
Robert D. Bolen
Fort Boise
Publishing Company

Dedication Page
I dedicate this work to Doris Anne,
the love of my life.

Contents

Contents..7.

Acknowledgements..9.

Foreword...11.

Chapter One

Idaho Indians..13.

Chapter Two

Explorers..31.

Chapter Three

Hudson's Bay Company..43.

Chapter Four

Indian Trade...57.

Chapter Five

Mountain Men..67.

Chapter Six

Wagons West..73.

Chapter Seven

Forts on the Oregon Trail..87.

Chapter Eight

Indian Wars...115.

Conclusion..171.

Index..172.

Bibliography..175.

Citing Electronic Publications...176.

About the Author..177.

Photo Courtesy Page.. 178.

Acknowledgements

I would like to thank Azusa Publishing.com for use of your wonderful postcards and Ned Eddins, author of Mountains of Stone, for great photos! I want to express my gratitude to George and Lise' Jumper for the Appaloosa pix and thanks to Bob Hubbard (Wyoming Trading Company) for the use of the Yellowstone and Teton Range postcards.

My thanks go to Jerry Fackrell, for the nice 16th Century Chevron Bead picture. I would like to express my appreciation to Allen Frank Owen for his editing. I am thankful to the Veteran's Administration for the photos of Fort Boise and my thanks to the Old Fort Boise Miniature Museum for the fort photo. I thank the Idaho Historical Society Library for your photo assistance in this work and to the Idaho State Historical Museum for pix of Sacajawea and the old houses.

A special thanks to Lerry Heath for the Three Island Crossing photo. Thank you to the Nevada Historical Society for the pictures of Sarah and Chief Winnemucca II. I want to thank the Library of Congress for the excellent wickiup photo. I give a special thank you to Len Sodenkamp for his unique artist's rendition of "Old Fort Boise" and Fort Hall. I would like to thank the Wal-Mart Photo staff for all of their countless hours of processing pictures.

Foreword

This book is a history of the discovery and possession of Northwestern America first by Native Indians and later by Europeans. The Snake River Indians arrived 3 or 4,000 years ago, some believe much earlier. The Norseman and Spanish Conquistadors came through early. They were followed by early explorers Lewis and Clark and the Hunt Astoria party, who opened the Northwest for passage. They passed through what became Idaho at the turn of the 19th Century.

During the Fur Trade Era the British Hudson's Bay Company expanded from Canada into what they called the Columbia District, which Americans later referred to as Oregon Country. This region was jointly owned by America and Britain at the time. John McLaughlin of the H.B.C. erected Fort Vancouver as headquarters for the Hudson's Bay Company and for trade with the Indians in 1824.

In 1834, the Hudson's Bay Company acquired Fort Boise and Fort Hall along the Snake River to trade furs with the local Indians. Settlements sprang up around the forts and teepees, too. Indians brought furs to the forts in trade for bright colored beads and other commodities. Mountain men trapped for furs and often took Indian women for brides, forming a bond. They lived off of the land like the Indian. With the Hudson's Bay Company's fur brigades, mountain men and Indians trapping furs, the beaver had become endangered and all but extinct in America by 1840.

In 1842 wagon trains began moving westward. Indians went on the warpath attacking the settlers and massacring the wagon trains. The President of the United States ordered the army out West. In 1848 the Columbia District became Oregon Territory. It contained the present day Idaho, Oregon, Washington, Montana and Wyoming, west of the Continental Divide.

The 1854 Ward Massacre and the Indian Wars of 1855 coupled with the erosion of the two forts by the Snake River caused both Fort Boise and Fort Hall in Idaho Territory to close in 1856.

With the western expansion blacksmiths, buffalo hunters, carpenters, Chinese rail workers, coopers, farmers, merchants, miners, sod busters and soldiers came west to Idaho Territory. Towns sprang up. Gold miners rushed to the area of new strikes and the white man poured onto Indian land by the thousands. Buffalo hunters killed thousands of buffalo for just their tongues and hides, hauled to the railhead and transported by the railroads. The senseless killing of the buffalo hurt the Indian. By the 1880's the bison, a major food source, had all but disappeared. The beaver were disappearing along with the buffalo. Western expansion brought disease to the Indian killing thousands.

As Indian Wars erupted a need for strong military garrisons was eminent. Major Pinckney Lugenbeel was ordered to build such a post in Idaho Territory, an extension of Fort Vancouver. Camp River Boise, later known as Fort Boise was erected in 1863 next to Boise City. With the Civil War winding down, Indian fighters arrived at the fort. The U.S. Army engaged the Indians in combat. One uprising was put down and another broke out, major Indian Wars ensued and the Amerindians were defeated. The Army began moving the Shoshoni Indians onto reservations in 1867. They confiscated the Indians' guns and shot their horses to limit movement. The last of the hostiles were moved onto reserves and it was over.

Chapter One
Idaho Indians

Seven tribes of American Indians dwelled in this area for hundreds of years before it became known as Idaho. The Northern Paiute, Bannock and Shoshoni were the southern tribes. The Nez Perce, Coeur d' Alene, Kalispell, and Kutenai were the Indian tribes in the North.

The Bannock, Paiute and Shoshoni tribes were called Snake Indians. Neighboring tribes referred to them, using the universal sign language of a slithering hand motion as snake. They described how the Snake Indians would disappear behind rocks like snakes.

Western Shoshoni bands were named for their dwelling places, like Boise, Bruneau, and the Weiser River Shoshoni. Over time Boise River and Bruneau River Shoshoni intermarried, becoming intermixed as one band. Northern Paiute or Numa (the people) and Western Shoshoni lived in the southwest. Bannock Indians lived farther east and the more eastern Fort Hall Shoshoni that dwelled near the fur fort intermarried creating the Shoshoni-Bannock people. The Bear River Shoshoni lived farther south and the Salmon River Shoshonis lived to the north.

Sororate polygyny (polygamy) was common among the Shoshoni. A man marrying an Indian bride also took her younger sisters for wives, and they all dwelled in the one lodge. Non-related wives had to reside in another lodge.

Shoshoni bands were composed of an extended family. Two or three generations of one family normally lived and traveled in one small band without a headman. Family bands combined with other families in a village or winter camp might have had a headman, who was social director of ceremonies, dances, festivals, hunts and war. The Indians

Snake Indian-"Heebee-Tee-Tse," a Shoshoni warrior was photographed by Rose & Hopkins-Denver, Colorado-1869. He is adorned in headdress, feathers, trade beads and otter fur in his braids.

Photo Courtesy of Azusa Publishing.com

Kalispell Indian maiden from the northern Idaho Territory panhandle is beautifully bedecked in seashells, shell earrings and necklace. Her braided hair has otter fur and weasel-skin dangles

Photo Courtesy of
Azusa Publishing.com

14

had no terminology for chief but books written about the Amerindian in English refer to a headman as chief to designate authority.

The headman was the dance director. The whole village participated. The Shoshoni held the Round Dance, War Dance and the Back and Forth Dance. The Scalp Dance was done mostly by women dancing around a scalp pole as the men drummed and played wooden rasps. Shoshonis caught young eagles and hawks and kept them in stick cages for their feathers that made headdresses and costumes which were worn in dance celebrations.

The Snake Indians were hunters and gatherers, with division of labor between the sexes. The men hunted and the women gathered. The women helped in fishing, picked berries, dug roots and gathered camas for flour to make bread. They trapped small rodents and gathered snakes, lizards and insects to eat, for instance, ground squirrel, rattler, horned toad, and grasshopper. Antelope, bear, buffalo, deer, elk, duck, geese, and rabbit were among the animals hunted by the men.

The Snake bands went from place to place gathering food in four seasonal cycles. Examples are salmon, buffalo, and mountain sheep. Combining salmon (agai), buffalo (k'utsun) or mountain sheep (tuka) with (deka'a) related eater of that food, as tukadeka'a (mountain sheep eater). The main diet of the Sheep-Eater Shoshoni was Rocky Mountain sheep. Meat from the mountain sheep was a solid staple for the Shoshoni Indians, similar to antelope, deer and buffalo. Lemhi and Salmon River Shoshonis that hunted these sheep thrived on this most nourishing meat.

They moved around as the season warranted. Winters were best spent in stream valleys protected from the wind. Deer, grouse, rabbit, sage hen and quail were also hunted for sustenance. Fish were caught through the ice. In the spring they went up into the foothills to harvest

15

the blue camas. Women dug camas roots and ground them in stone mortars into flour, baked into camas bread. In the summer they fished until the salmon season slowed in the fall.

At the end of summer, berries, nuts and seeds were gathered. The seeds were separated from the husks with beaters and collected into winnowing trays to separate out the chaff. Seeds were heated and dried for storage in cache pits. As autumn ended the Shoshoni band might return to their last winter haunt to begin again. Shoshonis dwelled near a creek, lake or river to access water for bathing, cooking or drinking. The women could draw water using pots or skins. A man leaving camp could carry a skin of water with him, like a modern canteen.

Women cooked, made pottery and grass baskets. An inventive method of cooking was with stones heated in a fire. They were transferred into a water-basket, sealed with pitch. As the water simmered meat was added to cook. Spits over the fire broiled meat. Firedogs were three slender flat rocks that supported a pot over a fire.

Northern Paiutes held communal drives to gather grasshoppers and Mormon crickets for food. The band formed a huge circle around a host of grasshoppers, closed in on the insects, ensnaring them in center nets. Rich in protein, grasshoppers were pounded in a mortar into pulp, roasted on a stick and eaten or pounded into flour to bake bread.

Grouse and rabbit drives were held. Jack rabbits were in abundance. It took about 200 rabbit skins to make a rabbit fur blanket. The fur covering made a warm, cozy blanket for sleeping in the winter time. Rabbits, mice and other rodents provided meat for the table. Jack rabbits multiplied at a rapid rate causing a population explosion an abundance of rabbits everywhere.

Herds of antelope ranged into the hundreds. The antelope is known for its speed. Its defense from predators is being able to run in an instant, reaching great speed before it is caught. The antelope hide was prized.

In smaller communal antelope drives, the band circled the desert deer, moving inward until the animal was ensnared to feed the whole family band. Drives for antelope, rabbits and sage hen were conducted in a similar manner.

Over a larger area, a communal antelope drive might have gone like this. The Indians would spread out over a great distance in a huge circle to encompass a large herd of antelope, completely surrounding the animals. The Indians used a corral and lanes of brush and rocks to drive the herd of antelope into the corral. The Snake Indians then slaughtered what they needed and freed the remainder.

Another method of hunting the antelope involved a shaman. Shaman magic was used to entice the antelope to come. The shaman used his magic to lure an antelope to come to him by hiding in the sagebrush and holding a bright colored cloth tied to a long stick high in the air. The antelope, being quite a curious animal, came up to the cloth and could be easily shot with bow and arrow, and shared by all. An Antelope Festival accompanied the antelope hunt with much festivity and dancing.

Buffalo in the Shoshoni language is k'utsun. Bison meat was prized. The walking Shoshoni located the bison herds to hunt. Hunting for them was an art. A brave crawling among the buffalo, concealed

The Indian cradle board allowed comfort for the papoose while the mother could use her hands to work. This cradle board was handcrafted by Justine L. Brown, daughter of Paiute Chief Louie.

(Courtesy Jackson Cramer)

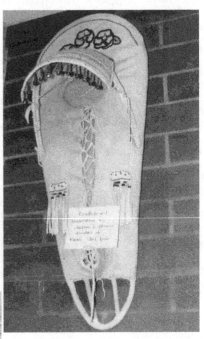

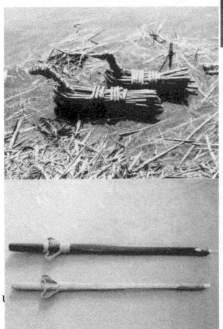

Top photo-Tule duck decoy replicas like the ones crafted by the Snake Indians, crafted by Kathy Hamlet. Bottom photo-exact atlatl replica made as the Indians did, courtesy master atlatl maker, Steve Sargent, Nampa, Idaho.

under a buffalo robe, could crawl among the buffalo. From that advantage point, he could get a clean shot with a bow and arrow. Often, a decoy buffalo was used to attract the herd could get a clean shot with a bow and arrow. Sometimes a decoy buffalo was used to attract a herd.

The communal Buffalo jump was an unusual technique of hunting. Lanes were built with rock barriers along the sides forming a kind of corral. A shaman would whoop and wave a blanket. The herd grazing near a cliff would spook and stampede over the edge, to be processed into meat and hides in butchering stations, used to process the bison. The whole band, shared the wealth. There was no waste. Skins made clothing, moccasins and teepees. Intestines were used for bindings and bowstrings. Hooves became spoons.

Deer were plentiful on the Snake River Plains. One deer would feed a small band for some time. The Indian being a conservative used all of the deer for one thing or the other. The hide was used for clothing and moccasins. Hooves made glue. Antlers were made into tools. The sinew was used to bind arrowheads to the arrow shafts and for sewing.

The moose at times were hunted. They are a large herbivore hunted mostly for the meat, though the Indians used its hide, bone and horn. Moose hides made warm clothing and the leather moccasins were more soft and supple than the buffalo leather.

With large herds in the region, elk was also an excellent food source for the Indians. The elk skin tanned hides was soft and made good moccasins and excellent leather clothing, as did deer. Indians used the bones for tools and their racks to make weapons.

Fishing was a big activity for the Shoshoni, as salmon swam upstream to spawn. Near Glenn's Ferry the Snakes used rocks to build

The Indian teepee was a tent constructed over numerous lodge poles in a conical shaped framework tied near the top, covered with buffalo skins, anchored with rocks at the base, with a mat or fur flooring.　　　　Courtesy of Azusa Publishing.com

The wickiup was a cone-shaped dwelling hut with upright poles, tied near the top and covered with bark or sewn matting overlay. Temporary brush huts were hastily made, covered with sagebrush and used for hunting.　　　　Courtesy of the Library of Congress

dams called weirs (still seen by air today) to trap salmon in the Snake River. With rock dams in place, the Shoshoni could fish by hand, use bone hooks, bow and arrow, nets, or spears. The Salmon-eaters fished the Snake River, east to Shoshone Falls and followed the migrating salmon, with a salmon-run in the spring and another in the fall.

Boise Shoshoni had a salmon fishery at the mouth of the Boise River yearly with plenty of salmon. They smoked large numbers of salmon on racks for drying and storage in cache pits for winter. Pemmican was smoked dried strips of salmon or meat and berries, especially chokecherries, with fat, ground in mortars, pressed into cakes, (saved in salmon skins) and cached in pits for winter.

The Boise Shoshoni Indians hosted their annual Salmon Festival where the Boise River flowed into the Snake River. The valley was a special meeting place for celebrating, dancing, festivals, fishing, gambling, horse racing, merry making, playing games and romance. It was called "Peace Valley." As the Salmon fest ended, the festivities carried over into their Trade Fair extravaganza.

The Shoshoni hosted fair was held on a large island at the confluence of the Boise, Malheur, Owyhee, Payette and Weiser Rivers with the Snake River near present day Payette. Peaceable Indians were welcomed from far and near in the celebrating, dancing, gambling music and trading arrow heads, arrows, bows, horses, knives, lodge-poles, obsidian, pelts, and other items.

The Indians found temporary refuge, taking advantage of natural caves, lava tubes, overhangs and rock shelters that made permanent or temporary shelters. The Paiutes and Shoshonis constructed pit houses that were built half above ground and half below ground, insulated from

21

the heat and cold. Walls of wooden poles were covered with earth and a roof of thatched rye grass. A hearth was used for heat and cooking.

The wickiup was a cone-shaped hut with upright poles, similar to the tipi. The frame hut was covered with bark, brush, or matting. The Snakes erected temporary dwellings in the hot high desert where they hunted and gathered food, called brush huts, with upright poles tied near the top, with sagebrush or branches for covering.

The Plains tipi (teepee) was sometimes called a wigwam. It was a tent constructed over numerous lodge poles in a conical shaped framework collapsible for travel. . It was tied near the top, covered with buffalo skins, anchored with rocks. Matting or hides made the flooring.

Another type of shelter was the Lemhi Shoshoni longhouse in the north. This dwelling was rectangular, partly underground. Walls were made of saplings lashed together and fastened to uprights with a thatch roof and the floor made of matting. These houses contained hearths.

The Snakes built communal sweat lodges, used by the men to socialize. Sweat baths were followed by a cold plunge. The Shoshoni walled up a running hot springs with stones making a permanent bath.

American Indians were healthy people, but due to severe winters and lack of food, many elderly people died of exposure and starvation.

A shaman led medicine bands that assisted him in warding off evil and healing illness. The Snakes believed in spirit guides and that all things animate or inanimate had life, even the sun, moon and stars. Such a belief was called animism. The eagle was a strong symbol for the Native American, when seen in his vision quests.

Hawk and eagle feathers made beautiful headdresses and costumes worn in dances, ceremonies and celebrations. Shoshonis caught young eagles and hawks and kept them in stick cages for their feathers.

The Snakes were great story tellers. Tales were told to all ages, using mythical animated characters, explaining creation and events in nature. Indian tales were told of colorful characters, such as Great Rabbit, Arrow Boy, Coyote, Children of the Sun and Star.

In the Creation story, Old Man Coyote made the world with the help of ducks. Ducks dove deep down in the water and found plant life. Coyote made people from the mud and made the Earth. Indians young and old loved the mythical stories.

Gaming was a favorite sport of the Shoshonis. They played stick games. Game-pieces were made of bone or stone. Guessing which hand behind the back held the game-stone was played. The boys drew a line in the dirt and lagged the piece to the line was another game. A game-piece was thrown; others would lag to try and hit the piece was also played. La Crosse and Chung-key were favorite games.

The atlatl was a throwing apparatus used in hunting large game as early as 13,000 B.P. The spear had an 8 inch fore-shaft with spearhead and hollow reed or wooden shaft. The spear was thrown by way of a strap on a wooden thruster with finger-loops and a hook for the spear at elbows' length. A weight might added to the underside for momentum. The atlatl could be thrown for 100 yards, to bring down big game, such as mammoth and bison-bison.

After the atlatl came the bow and arrow in the last 2,000 years. The Snake Indians crafted fine bows and arrows, which were admired by other tribes. A shaft was heated and straightened, smoothed and polished for an arrow. Indians flint knapped (chipped) arrow heads from chert or obsidian and inserted them into a slit in the end of the shaft, glued with pitch and wrapped with sinew. Bow strings were made from animal gut. Eagle, hawk or similar feathers were used to fletch an arrow.

Spanish explorers brought the first modern horses from Spain to the American Continent. The Ute Indians stole horses from them early on. The Utes thought horses to be big dogs. They were the first Indians to acquire horses in America. Cortez imprisoned Utes in the 1500's for stealing horses forcing them to work in the gold and silver mines.

The Comanche Indians were Shoshoni Indians that had migrated from Wind River in 1500 A.D., into Nebraska, then south into Kansas, Oklahoma and continued south into northern Texas, where the lodged.

The Apaches raided the Spanish colonists in the late 1600's, stealing horses. It was regarded as an act of bravery for the Comanche to slip in at night and steal horses from the Apaches.

Although the Comanche Indians had the horse after the Apache and Ute Indians they became the most expert horsemen and the fiercest warriors of any tribe of Indians of the Plains. The Comanche would ride after Ute horsemen who were hunting buffalo on the Plains and scare them off scattering their camps. They loved their horses and sang songs to them. Horses were groomed and their tails braided. If a Comanche warrior died, his horses were all killed and buried with him.

In the 1700's the Comanche drove horses up to Fort Hall to their Shoshoni cousins, trading horses at the Shoshoni held Trade Fairs. The Boise River Shoshoni were one of the first Snake bands to acquire horses. Their horses grazed on the plush green grasses of the Boise River bottoms where there was good drinking water. This bottom land along

Ute Indians stole horses from the Spaniard and by the late 1600's entered into slave trade with them. With the horse and the element of surprise ruthless Ute Indians took slaves of unsuspecting Navajo, Plains Indians and neighboring Shoshoni. (Photo Courtesy of Azusa Publishing, L.L.C.)

Chief Joseph's Nez Perce Tribe adopted the beautiful Appaloosa horse as their favorite one to breed, a strong stock obtained from the Comanche Indians. The Nez Perce raised splendid Appaloosa horses.   (Photo Courtesy of Jumper Horse/Sport)

the Boise River was called Peace Valley, in Shoshoni (Cop-cop-pa-ala) meaning Cottonwood Feast Valley. The Nez Perce also acquired the Appaloosa, their favorite breed of horse, from the Comanche tribe.

The Horse and Indian Era allowed the American Indian the freedom of movement in war or to travel great distance in the hunt of the buffalo. The horse provided their mode of daily transportation. The style of living with the horse suited the American Indian and will always be remembered in their hearts and minds. The Indian proved to be excellent horse handlers and raisers.

Horses hauled their goods and provided many a good horse race. After the Indians acquired horses, they used them to pull and drag two poles called a travois. Hides to cover a teepee, goods and infants were hauled this way. With additional poles the Indians constructed a teepee.

As the young brave became a man, he learned to count coup. The brave would run or ride at a gallop toward his opponent, giving war-whoops, strike him with his quirt, then depart, proving bravery by getting in his enemies' face. This practice changed with actual warfare that could mean loss of life. Scalping was learned from the French and many scalps were taken. The custom spread throughout the tribes.

In prehistoric days, millions of buffalo roamed the Great Plains. Buffalo populations were known to graze as far west as the base of the Blue Mountains. Now, the bison populations had dwindled on the Snake River Plain. Shoshoni horsemen had to travel farther to find buffalo. In autumn, Horse-mounted Shoshoni made their annual journey to the upper Missouri to hunt buffalo. Buffalo was at the top of the food chain for the Plains Indians. Hunting the buffalo became an industry. Pack mules were taken on the expedition to haul the buffalo meat and robes home.

Top photo-The buffalo was the top of the food chain for the Shoshoni Indian. (Author photo)

Bottom photo-Rocky Mountain Sheep were the main staple of The Sheep-eater Shoshoni. (Photo Courtesy of Ned Eddins)

Top Photo-Elk an excellent food source and the elk skin tanned hides were soft leather and made superb moccasins and clothing, as did deer. (Photo Courtesy of Ned Eddins)

Bottom photo-Desert deer, the high desert pronghorn antelope was a good food source for the Indians. they hunted them by various methods. (Author photo)

The Shoshoni, like other tribes, learned early that traveling to Montana could mean being attacked by fierce Blackfeet or Crow Indians. They rode in greater numbers invading enemy territory and were careful crossing enemy lands.

The Mountain Crow dwelled in the Bighorn Valley, while the River Crow lodged along the flowing headwaters of the Yellowstone River in Montana.

Mounted Shoshoni also made the trek across Blackfeet territory in order to reach the buffalo. Their biggest threat was the fierce Blackfeet Indians. Picture a long line of silent Shoshonis on horseback passing single file, undetected through Blackfeet and Crow country. At any time, bands of enemy Indians might attack them.

Blackfeet war parties might raid anytime they thought they could acquire Shoshoni ponies. The Shoshonis kept a constant vigil for them. The Blackfeet warred on neighboring tribes and were hated by them. They were called the Blackfeet because their moccasin soles were blackened walking across the burned prairie.

For their own preservation, the Snake River tribes, like the Plateau, formed militant hunting parties in large numbers of socio-political allies to hunt bison. Shoshoni hunting parties were made up of Bannock, Eastern Shoshonis, Flathead and Paiute allies. They had a fighting chance of getting the needed buffalo and not losing their scalps.

Buffalo hunters followed the bison onto the Plains. Riding at a gallop alongside a fleeing buffalo, a Snake brave could shoot an arrow between its ribs, penetrating a lung, and drop the beast. Shoshoni bow hunters killed enough buffalo for their family. The hunter rode alongside a buffalo and with a few quick jabs of his lance dropped the buffalo.

Indian Travois- A horse pulled and drug two poles called a travois. Hides, goods and infants could be hauled this way. The travois was collapsible. With additional poles a teepee (tipi) could be erected   Photo Courtesy of Azusa Publishing, L.L.C.

Kutenai Indian gathers reeds from his canoe in Northern Idaho country. Using a willow frame the Kutenai constructed crude boats used to fish or cross rivers. Duck decoys were fashioned of reeds for hunting. Photo Courtesy of Azusa Publishing, L.L.C.

Horses brought immense change to the Indian life-way. For 150 years horses would revolutionize the Amerindians' world. They loved their ponies, but the romance between the horse and Indian was short lived. Palefaces coming marked the end of the "Horse and Indian Era."

From the time the Indians migrated onto the continent they had possessed of the land without ownership, since their religion and belief system didn't allow it. The American Indians had use of the land, yet never intended to own it. For thousands of years they dwelled here; it was in their care. White explorers began arriving in Indian country.

The white man had a different philosophy about land ownership and soon their wagon trains dotted the horizon followed by thousands of miners, railroad workers, buffalo hunters and the U.S. Army Cavalry.

~~~~~~~~~~

During historic times, in Idaho Territory, Indian characters among the Shoshoni tribe became famous. Sacajawea, Chiefs: Cameawait, Eagle-Eye, Peime, Pocatello, Ten Doy, and Washakie made history. Bannock Chiefs Buffalo Horn and Egan were notorious in war. Heroes in the Nez Perce Indian tribe Chiefs Joseph and his Sub-chiefs Lawyer, Looking Glass, Ollicut, Moxmox (Yellow Wolf), White Bird and Yellow Bull made fame. Among the Northern Paiute tribe mostly in Nevada Territory, Chiefs Truckee, Winnemucca, his daughter, Sarah and Wavoka were popular figures. Sioux Indians on the northern border of Idaho Territory, (enemies of the Snake Indians) known for their fame and leadership during warfare with the U.S. 7th Cavalry were Chiefs: Crazy Horse, Gall, Sitting Bull, Spotted Tail, Rain-In-the-Face and Red Cloud. All of these were great Sioux chiefs who battled the Blue-coats.

~~~~~~~~~~

Chapter Two
Explorers

In the Seventeenth Century Europeans began arriving in North America east of the Mississippi. Western America remained a wilderness. In 1800, few American had been west of the Mississippi. At the turn of the 19th Century the western frontier was still a wilderness, inhabited mostly by Indians and animals. Jefferson became President in 1801 and sent a message in secret to Congress urging that trade be established with the Indians. He would urge them to raise livestock, grow crops and enter into manufacturing. In 1803 the territory west of the Mississippi to the Rocky Mountains between Canada and Mexico was obtained from France in the Louisiana Purchase, for $15,000, 000. Jefferson was interested in the land west of the Rockies to the Pacific Ocean. He asked Congress for monies for the mission. Congress responded with a mere $2500 to bankroll an expedition.

President Thomas Jefferson authorized the military expedition of Captain Meriwether Lewis and Captain Clark in 1803 of the Corp of Discovery with 31 army corps and hired men cross-country to the Pacific Ocean opening up a whole new hemisphere of western expansion.

The Corp journeyed from St. Louis to the upper Missouri River Valley region of what is now North Dakota. Lewis and Clark reached the Sioux speaking, Mandan Village on the north bank of the Missouri River. At that time, Toussaint Charbonneau, a French-Indian fur trapper, greeted them. They hired him as interpreter and met his wife, Sacajawea or "Bird Woman," in the Shoshoni language.

The Lewis and Clark party spent the winter of 1804-1805 in Fort Mandan. Sacajawea bore Charbonneau a son, named Baptiste. They left

Buffalo beneath the Tetons- In the spring, the Shoshoni Kutsundeka'a (buffalo eaters) crossed to the upper Missouri to hunt buffalo in Montana Territory and followed the buffalo to the Plains. The buffalo was top of the food chain (Courtesy N.E.)

Appaloosa colt- Shoshonis and Plains Indians had the Appaloosa horse as well as the Nez Perce. The Nez Perce bred them into fine stock. During the Nez Perce War Chief Joseph ran as many as 2,000 head.   Courtesy of Jumper Horse/Sport

Fort Mandan and canoed the Missouri through "grizzly country", to its headwaters in the spring of 1805.

The Corp descended the western slopes of the Rocky Mountains. Low on supplies, they counted on reaching Sacajawea's people for help. "Fort Colt Killed Camp" was the site (1805), where Lewis and Clark were forced to kill a young colt to keep them from starvation.

Sacajawea began to recognize landmarks of the high mountain valley haunt of her people. Gradually Shoshoni Indians became visible as their camp was reached. Recognizing her brother, she rushed to Chief Cameahwait and began sucking her fingers, the Shoshoni sign of kinship. The reunion was a gala affair!

Sacajawea spoke no English, only Shoshoni and Hidatsa dialects. She and her husband worked as a team. She translated Shoshoni into the Hidatsa tongue. Charbonneau knew Hidatsa and translated the message into French. There was a French speaker in the party who spoke English.

Lewis and Clark sat cross-legged and traded with the Shoshoni. Clark was able to get provisions, pack horses and guides from them. Canoes were cached for the return trip by sinking them with good sized rocks. Horses were used for further travel.

The party camped in Nez Perce country, to build additional dugout canoes. This site was called "Canoe Camp." Trees were felled along the river for dugout canoes, fashioned from logs, as needed. They found passage through the Rocky Mountains, by canoeing the Clearwater River to the Snake River and from the Snake to the Columbia and on to the Pacific Ocean.

The statue of Sacajawea stands at the entrance to the Idaho State Historical Museum downtown Boise, Idaho. Sacajawea was famous for her role in the Lewis and Clark Expedition to the Pacific Ocean, when her husband Charbonneau, a French fur trapper, signed on as interpreter with Lewis and Clark. As a teenager, Sacajawea, a Lemhi Shoshoni, was taken captive by the Hidatsa Indians. Charbonneau won Sacajawea in a gambling game with them and took her as his third wife, in Indian tradition.

Author photo

Sacajawea canoed with her papoose in a cradle board, strapped to her back. Once the boat swamped and Sacajawea saved several precious parcels. She was very ill on the trip for about a week.

It was a perilous 8,000 mile venture over rugged terrain, traveling to the Pacific Ocean and back. In what is now Idaho, Lewis and Clark also contacted the Nez Perce Indians. They traded guns and ammunition for horses. The Nez Perce provided a great feast with gifts for the explorers, who were given safe passage through their country. "Long Camp or Camp Chopunnish," in East Kamiah, was where the party waited until spring to cross the snow-covered mountains. On their return trip from the Pacific, Sacajawea turned out to be a huge asset to Clark on the journey and was honored for her achievements.

In August of 1804, Pierre Dorion (also spelled Dorian) Jr. was introduced to Lewis and Clark along the Missouri by his father, Pierre Dorion Sr. who worked as interpreter for Lewis and Clark and was friends with Clark's brother. Pierre Dorion Jr. had been trapping on the James River and trading with the Yankton Sioux Indians at the time.

An Iowa Sioux Indian, Marie was born in a teepee on the banks of the Missouri River. She married Pierre Dorion, Jr., a French-Sioux Indian cross who spoke Sioux. Hunt needed a Sioux interpreter and they were scarce. In 1810 Dorion was interpreter for the Manuel Lisa party on the Missouri, but drank too much. (1811) He signed on with Wilson Price Hunt's party of fur traders in St. Louis, as interpreter with the pact that his family go along on the expedition.

The Pierre and Marie Dorion family departed St. Louis with the Hunt Party embarking up the Missouri River in dugout canoes, reaching an Arikara Indian village (1811). Canoes at that time were cached. Hunt

35

bartered with the Arikaras for horses. Traveling by horseback, they met Crow Indians, with whom he traded for horses. A Crow Chief sent a thieving white man, named Edward Rose to guide them across the Bighorn Mountains to the Wind River in Wyoming Territory.

In 18 days the Hunt group reached the Cheyenne Indians, where he traded again for new mounts. White Pinto horses with red or black blotches were called Indian ponies, the favorite horses of many Plains Indians because of their unusual colorations. The Cheyenne were trade partners with the Arikaras.

The party crossed Union Pass turning southwest to the Green River valley, where they hunted buffalo and jerked two tons of meat. Shoshoni Indians traded them another ton of jerky. Crossing the Hobart River Valley Basin, they reached the Snake River, where they began to build dugout canoes from cottonwoods. After exploring it, Reed determined that the terrain was not crossable.

They crossed the Continental Divide and continued on southwest to Jackson's Hole and hiked out of the Teton Range. Four trappers remained to trap beaver near Three Forks. A Crow Indian raiding party killed one of the trappers in the spring of 1812.

Two Snake Indians guided them across the Snake River, up Fall Creek and over Teton Pass, crossing the Continental Divide to Pierre's Hole. The party acquired dugout canoes and continued down the North Fork of the Snake River to Henry's Fork. One man drowned and the party lost canoes at Caldron Lynn. Hiking the Snake River Canyon into Idaho, Marie suffered from exhaustion, exposure, hunger and thirst. They had trouble navigating the rivers and hiked three days without water. The

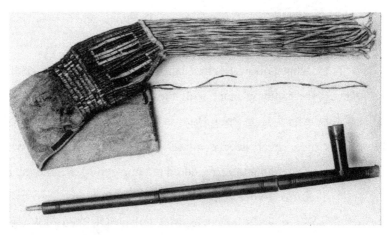

Indian peace pipe and bag- Captains Lewis and Clark sat cross-legged and smoked the pipe with the Shoshonis to show friendship. They also traded for horses.

Courtesy of the Idaho State Historic Library

Old Drawing of Nez Perce-Lewis and Clark met with the Nez Perce Indians. They smoked the peace pipe and traded with them. They were given presents by these Indians and safe passage through their land

Courtesy of the Idaho State Historic Library

party reached Hagerman Valley in Idaho Territory, where they finally found drinking water. Hunt's party had made it over the Rockies!

Near what is now Eagle, Idaho they came upon Snake Indians, who shared fresh puppy meat with them. The first white man in the Boise Valley was Wilson Price Hunt in 1811. Pierre Dorion traded with the Indians for a much needed horse. Marie braved the trek with two infants; he dismounted and surrendered the horse to Marie and the boys.

The Astor Expedition split into three groups led by Hunt, McKenzie and Crooks. McKenzie, McClellan and Reed took the north route through Lewiston and floated the Snake to the Columbia and on to Fort Astoria, arriving on January 18, 1812.

Hunt's group trekked west over the Snake River Plain. Hunt bartered for canoes from the Wishram Indians at the mouth of the Walla-Walla and arrived at Astoria, February 15, 1812. Crooks and Ramsey took the south route later to be rescued on the bank of the Columbia, starved and half-naked and reached the fort on May 11, 1812, uniting the group. Astoria risked fur shipments to England during the War of 1812.

One year later (1813), Pierre and Marie were back at the mouth of the Boise River working for Reed (also Reid), of the Astoria Fur Trade Group. Reed traded for horses to traverse the Snake River Plain.

His party consisted of Chapelle, Delaunay, Dorion (and family), Landry, Le Clerc, and Turcot. Reed rescued lost trappers, Hoback, Rezner and Robinson, who joined his group. Landry and Turcot died; Delaunay disappeared. It was feared that he was scalped.

Reed created trading camps along the Boise River. "Reed's Post" was erected in 1813 as a winter trading post just south of the Boise

Left view Yellowstone Grand Canyon Lower falls-The Clark Party traveled along the colorful Yellowstone River when Captain William Clark explored the area.

Right view Grand Tetons-Lewis and Clark and the Hunt Party traveled through the Tetons.   (Courtesy Bob Hubbard)

Sun peeks through mountains at Jackson Hole- They crossed the Continental Divide and southwest to Jackson's Hole (Courtesy N.E.)

River east of the Snake at the mouth of the Boise River. Andre La Chapelle, Giles Le Clerc, Pierre Dorion and Jacob Rezner used a cabin (hut or lean-to) Reed built for lodging where beaver were plentiful.

Reed had deserted the first cabin at the Fort Boise location. Uunruly Indians often came demanding guns. In 1814, a band of warring Bannocks, up to no good, burned down the abandoned cabin and continued down the Boise giving war-whoops and singing songs of war.

Marie was skinning beaver at Reed's new shelter, 15 miles east of the first cabin, on the north side of the Boise River, in the settlement of Notus, in the Boise River Valley. A friendly squaw informed her that the warring Dog-ribs Indians were headed up river toward her. Marie instantly lashed her boys to her horse and headed up stream to find Pierre. It became dark and she camped for the night. It was stormy the next morning so Marie waited there. The next day she saw smoke, possibly a smoke signal from the Indians so she remained there.

On the third day, Marie found Le Clerc mortally wounded. He told her that hostiles had massacred the Reed party and that her husband was dead. Marie hoisted the wounded man onto her horse, but he could barely ride and kept falling off. Marie headed for the main cabin.

As she approached, Marie saw Indians gallop off, near the ford of the river. Le Clerc died and Marie buried him as best she could with snow and brush. She reached the main cabin and found Pierre, Reed, and the others murdered, scalped and mutilated.

The children were now cold and hungry so she built a fire for them. Marie returned to the cabin, armed only with her knife and a tomahawk. On the way, Marie saw wolves eating their kill, so she scared them off. She found a fresh supply of fish in the cabin and hurried back

Jean Baptist Charbonneau, Sacajawea's son was buried in Oregon south of Jordan Valley on May 18, 1866. He was the youngest member of the Corps of Discovery.   Author photo

William Clark's Signature- Captain Clark went south to explore the Yellowstone as Captain Lewis journeyed north to the Marias River. Clark and 13 men on horse-back traveled into Yellowstone, where he discovered Pompey's Pillar. Clark carved his name on a sandstone bluff he named Pomp's Tower (Courtesy N.E.)

to the boys. Stoking the fire and adding more wood, she cooked the fish and they ate for the first time in three days. Here, she rested a few days with her sons before attempting to travel.

Marie packed her horse and with children and supplies, crossed the Snake River and headed for the Pacific and Fort Astoria, forging west for nine days. She crossed the snow-covered Blue Mountains. She and the boys waited out the winter under an overhang, (near a mountain stream). Marie built a crude lean-to from brush, pine blows and snow. They survived on bits of horseflesh, berries and small rodents; wolves threatened and when the rations ran out, Marie killed her horse for food.

She carried Paul in an Indian cradleboard on her shoulders and took Baptiste's hand trekking over the Blues. They trudged on, crossing the Plains along the Walla-Walla River. The next day Marie reached the summit, snow-blind and tired out; the Walla-Walla Indians rescued them.

Marie and Sacajawea had once met in 1811, when the Manual Lisa Party overtook the Hunt party. The famous heroines had much in common. Both Marie Dorion and Sacajawea were American Indians. Marie was married to Pierre Dorion, Jr., a French-Indian cross, while Sacajawea married Toussaint Charbonneau, a French-Indian cross.

Their husbands were French Canadian Mountain Men, fur traders and interpreters for worked as interpreter for Lewis and Clark Sacajawea had sons named Baptiste and crossed America from St. Louis to the Pacific with famous explorers. The two brought their infants along on their journey. Their husbands were Pierre's father, Pierre Dorion Sr.

Both of these famous women in American History led very similar lives. Marie Dorion remarried twice and lived out her new life in Oregon Territory raising a family. She died September 5, 1850.

Chapter Three
Hudson's Bay Company

Jacques Carter began fur trapping and trading with the Indians near Montreal, Canada in the St. Lawrence River Valley, giving the French a foothold in the North American fur trade. Henry Hudson discovered the 475,000 square mile inland sea in 1599, engulfing one third of Canada, to be known as Hudson Bay. This Arctic region was rich in beaver and other fur bearers, seal, walrus and whales.

In 1665 King Charles enlisted two French fur trappers and equipped them with two ships. One of them, the Nonesuch, made it to the Hudson Bay and returned with a meager shipload of beaver pelts in 1669, inspiring the King to commission the English Company of Adventurers, known as the Hudson's Bay Company (H.B.C.) They wrote their charter covering the fur trade on all the rivers in Northern Canada, with safe passage from King Charles and Canada's Monarch, Prince Rupert. With their own processing plants, ships and a good infrastructure the company had rapid growth and built an empire covering the Western Hemisphere. They set up headquarters in the frigid Arctic region on the Hudson and James Bays for trade with the Cree Indians, with abundant furs. Some commodities provided by-products such as goose quills, walrus tusks, bear grease, and whale oil. 100,000 seal skins were taken per year from 1670-1870. Two American firms, the XYZ, the John Jacob Astor Companies and the Northwest Fur Company of Montreal were HBC's strongest competitors.

The Hudson's Bay Company merged with the Northwest Company and expanded into America. They would eventually buy out the other two rivals. Their center of trade was in the upper Mississippi region. Headquarters in the Northwest was established in Oregon Territory, included Idaho, Oregon, Washington, western Montana and Wyoming, also much of British Columbia.

The French were competed with fiercely in the fur trade. The French and Indian War broke out between the French with their Indian allies, (the Algonquian and the Huron Indians) and Britain.

DR. JOHN MᶜLOUGHLIN.

Dr. John McLaughlin, a Scot, was the founder of Fort Vancouver, headquarters for the Hudson's Bay Company in the Northwest and Oregon City. Chief Factor. McLaughlin was in charge of 34 outposts, 24 ports, six ships, and 600 employees. He was called, "the Father of Oregon." He founded Oregon City (Courtesy I.H.S.L.)

Americans entered the fur trade along the upper Ohio Valley. Their expansion was blocked by the French during the war. English ships were attacked by French warships in Hudson Bay. British ports and other forts were seized by the French. When the war concluded, the French awarded land back to England. This included Newfoundland and Nova Scotia.

Trapping beaver was an art. The trapper looked for fallen trees, a gnawed tree trunk or a beaver dam. A bait stick smeared with the sex gland of a beaver was hung over a strong metal trap and set inches below water's surface. A chain ran from the trap to a stake secured in deeper water. A caught beaver drowned by the weight of the heavy trap. Traps were checked regularly and beaver were removed, skinned and bundled.

Captain Gray, American commander of the "Columbia," sailing ship was a trader along the Puget Sound and Washington coast. He traded for furs with the coastal Indians. In 1792, Gray discovered the mouth of the Columbia River and sailed up river for several miles.

Great Britain, France and Spain all created interests in the Pacific Northwest. On October 20, 1818 Britain signed a treaty with the United States to jointly occupy the Northwest Territory for ten years. Early in 1819 Spain ceded her right to the territory of Idaho, Oregon and Washington. Russia ceded all her rights to the Northwest region in 1824. In 1828 Britain renewed a ten year agreement.

In the fall of 1810, Hudson's Bay Company factor, Jacob House built "Fort Howse" on Flathead Lake's north end in Montana Territory for the North West Company. When Hudson's Bay Company bought out the North West firm, Montana Territory proved to be a good beaver hunting area.

McKenzie held a trade rally with his trappers, the Bannock and Shoshoni Indians. Meeting with Chief Peiem and other chiefs, McKenzie paved the way for trapping in the region. He reached the Indians in remote regions on snowshoes, when the snow was excessively deep.

Donald McKenzie had been employed by the Astoria Fur, North West and Hudson's Bay Companies. He crossed over the Blue Mountains with a trapping expedition of 55 men and 195 horses fully equipped with 300 traps, rations and supplies. McKenzie left six Iroquois Indians at temporary Fort Boise with food, traps and gear. He positioned trapping camps for the best fur hunting. McKenzie took a beaver brigade in boats, up the Snake River dropping off trappers, as far as the Bear River. Later, he returned to "Fort Boise" to find that the Iroquois had scattered to local Indian villages.

Norman Kittson's expedition from Fort Nez Perce had been delayed and McKenzie sent a crew of ten men to intercept them. Indians had stolen their horses. They were found and their stolen horses recovered from the Indians. They reunited at temporary Fort Boise. McKenzie held a rendezvous there in 1819. A year later he held peace talks on the Little Lost River with the Shoshoni.

The Northwest Company and the Hudson's Bay Company rivaled American fur companies in the Snake River region. Employees, Peter Scene Ogden, Alexander Ross and John Work trapped the Snake River Plain in the early 1800's. In 1823 Alexander Ross erected "Flathead Post," called the Second Salish House, five miles east of Thompson Falls, in Flathead country. He endured severe winters deep in Montana Territory. Ross's beaver brigade of 140 men, with Iroquois Indians skins entered Idaho's Salmon River country reaping over 5,000 beaver skins.

46

Beaver dam- Finding fallen or gnawed trees or a beaver dam was the first trick. A strong metal trap was set below the water's surface with a chain to a stake secured the trap in deeper water. The caught beaver drowned. Beaver were skinned and bundled   (Courtesy N. E.)

Whitman Spalding Oregon Trail Marker- These Missionaries came over land from New York to Fort Boise in 1836, the first wagon to cross the plains. The wagon broke down there and was abandoned at the fort. Mrs. Spalding and Whitman were the first white women to reach Oregon (Courtesy N. E.)

Peter Scene Ogden replaced Ross in the field, serving from 1824-1831 for the Hudson's Bay Company as beaver brigade leader into the Snake River drainage. Brigade leaders James W. Dease and John Work were added in the field because of the rich trapping yields in the Snake River region. Brigade leader, John Work, traded out of Fort Nez Perce. Work became renowned as a Hudson's Bay trader working with the Blackfoot and Salish Indians in the field. Items exchanged for furs were axes, beads, blankets, pipes, coffee, guns, knives, mirrors and tobacco.

The Amerindian manufactured beads of bone, horn, and shell, stone and wood for centuries and commerce was lucrative among the Indian natives. Before the arrival of trade goods to the Indians, The Shoshoni had their own trade centers as did the Cheyenne, Crow, Mandan, Nez Perce.' Trade routes crossed the Pacific Northwest.

A list of goods stocked in Hudson's Bay trade posts in 1670 were beads, brass rings, burning glasses, calico shirts, coats, caps, gunpowder, kersey cloth (red & blue), kettles, knives, lace, powder horns, red Gloucester, scimitars, thread, tinsel, twine and yarn stockings.

Stock from Hudson's Bay Company Fur Trade Posts Company, and the American Fur Company included numerous varieties of glass, shell, and stone beads of trade were bartered or sold in stores of fur trade posts. The Hudson's Bay Company was a highly successful operation.

By 1826 the monopoly covered about three million square miles and employed some 1500 people around the world. The Hudson's Bay Company was the oldest corporation in North America.

The Northwest Territory at this time was co-owned by America and Britain. A Scot, Dr. John McLoughlin was the founder of Fort Vancouver headquarters for the Hudson's Bay Company in the

Northwest and Oregon City. He was commissioned General Manager to build "Fort Vancouver," in 1825 on the north bank of the Columbia River, the center of trade in the western hemisphere. Chief Factor. McLoughlin was in charge of 34 outposts, 24 ports, six ships, and 600 employees. Company records were kept in English at the head table though the trade language was pidgin. The Hudson's Bay Company Headquarters in the Northwest was based at Fort Vancouver.

The palisade was built with 750' x 450' x 20' walls. There were 40 buildings: a blacksmith shop, chapel, housing, and warehouses. Outside of the ramparts was a residential village, called Kanaka, where many Hawaiians resided. Other employees were French Canadian, Chelas, Cree, Irish, Iroquois and Scot peoples. Included was a dairy, distillery, fields, fruit orchards, a garden, sawmill, ship yard and tannery.

During the 1820's brigades of Hudson's Bay trappers pushed south from Vancouver, along the Siskiyou trail, into the San Francisco Bay Region. By the 1830's the English group had control of the fur trade in Oregon country. Hudson's Bay Company chose the uncharted region that would become Idaho as the site for their fur trade fort. They monopolized the fur trade leaving their mark on American history.

As in Canada, supplies were brought in to ocean ports and up rivers to reach the Hudson's Bay Company forts. A practice of the company was to trade bright colored woolen blankets to the Indians for furs. These were called Hudson's Bay point blankets.

During the Fur Trade Era Beaver skin top-hats became the rage in England, as beaver trade came to a close in 1870, top-hats took its place. On May 20, 1843 the Provisional Government was established in Oregon Territory and Abernathy was made Governor.

49

French trappers named the river, "Riviera Bois" or Boise River, bois meaning wooded area, the source of the name, Boise, in early Idaho. The Boise River was used by the Shoshoni Indians and French trappers for years. French traders named other local rivers such as the Malheur, Weiser and the Payette River was named for Captain Francois Payette.

In the fall of 1832, Captain Nathaniel J. Wyeth arrived at Fort Vancouver. He made a trip back East in 1833, returning overland from Boston with three missionaries, Indian Agent White and a few Indians. They were well received by Doctor McLoughlin. The Doctor was a very charitable and generous man. He yielded a lot of responsibility in the Hudson's Bay Company. In 1834 McLoughlin would send McKay into the Snake River Region to build Fort Snake (Fort Boise). In 1834, Wyeth received a shipload of merchandise, chickens, goats and sheep. He created a post for trading and trapping on an island at the junction of the Willamette River and the Columbia Rivers, called Wapato.

Missionaries, Marcus and Narcissa Prentiss Whitman with Henry and Eliza Spalding traveled overland from New York, reaching Fort Boise, in 1836. Whitman's was the first wagon to cross the plains and abandoned the broken down remnant at the fort. They were escorted on to "Fort Walla-Walla" and "Fort Vancouver" by Hudson's Bay Company employees. They were the first white women in Oregon. (1836).

Reverend Henry Spalding established Lapwai Mission Station, Idaho's first settlement among the Nez Perce, 12 miles north of Lewiston, on the Clearwater River. He imported a printing Press to print the New Testament into the Nez Perce language. The same year Marcus established the Whitman Presbyterian Mission for the Cayuse Indians, 25 miles east of Fort Walla-Walla. He also established another mission at

50

Kamiah, 50 miles southeast of Lapwai. Whitman and Spalding brought wagon loads of supplies to their missions from Green River, Wyoming, establishing a wagon route to Fort Walla-Walla.

Rev. Whitman promised the Cayuse Indians monies for land (1835) that was never paid. The Cayuse vandalized the mission. In 1842 Indian Agent White arrived with more emigrants without soldiers for protection, money or goods for them.

Later that year the American Board of Commissioners for Foreign Missions decided to close the Oregon Missions. In October Whitman started back East to try and keep the missions open, crossing the Blue Mountains reaching Fort Hall, Fort Benton and Santa Fe. In 1843 he joined a trading company, en route to St. Louis.

Rev. Whitman reached the East to seek monies, but was advised to abandon the idea. Whitman sold his New York home to raise money. He left New York on horseback with pack animals. Reaching the Platte River in Nebraska Territory, Marcus Whitman joined emigrants bound for Fort Walla-Walla heading up a massive wagon-train into Oregon in 1843. Hundreds of emigrants followed.

Dr. Whitman wrote to James Porter, Secretary of War, saying he had piloted one thousand settlers with 120 wagons, 700 oxen and 800 cattle to Oregon in 1843. They stopped at Fort Boise and purchased coffee and flour from the Hudson Bay's Company at $50 dollars per hundred pounds, spending $2,000.00, a good price.

Whitman's Mission was on Cayuse Indian land near thousands of Indians. In his absence, they attacked the mission, burned down a grist mill and other buildings, while the Nez Perce demonstrated at Lapwai. Mrs. Whitman had fled to Fort Walla-Walla during the attack and later

Serpentine side-plates-These same serpent side-plates or lock-plates were embossed on a North West trade gun from the Fur Trade Era. The side-plates were found in the southeast Oregon high desert. The lock-plates are certainly museum worthy and a lucky find.

The side-plate photo is from the David Brooks collection.

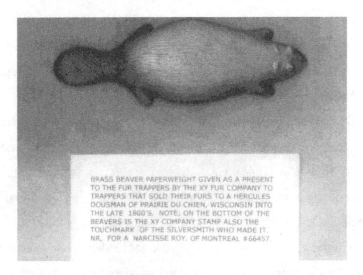

BRASS BEAVER PAPERWEIGHT GIVEN AS A PRESENT TO THE FUR TRAPPERS BY THE XY FUR COMPANY TO TRAPPERS THAT SOLD THEIR FURS TO A HERCULES DOUSMAN OF PRAIRIE DU CHIEN, WISCONSIN INTO THE LATE 1800'S. NOTE; ON THE BOTTOM OF THE BEAVERS IS THE XY COMPANY STAMP ALSO THE TOUCHMARK OF THE SILVERSMITH WHO MADE IT. NR, FOR A NARCISSE ROY, OF MONTREAL #66457.

Actual brass paper weight given by the XY Fur Company in the 1800' to their fur trappers that sold furs to a Hercules Dousman of Prairie Du Chien, Wisconsin. Artifact is from the Bill Ross collection John Day, Oregon.   Author photo was escorted back home by Hudson's Bay Company employees after Rev Whitman arrived in early autumn of 1843.

A peacemaker, Indian Agent White and H.B.C. employees spoke to the Cayuse and continued on to Lapwai to parley with the Nez Perce chiefs. They smoked the peace-pipe, signing a peace treaty. Agent White gave the Indians garden tools to appease them. White went back to "Fort Dalles" and on to Astoria to make peace with discontented Indians.

In 1846, Great Britain signed a treaty with the President of the United States giving America land south and west of the Rocky Mountains to the Pacific Ocean. The 49th parallel was made the boundary between Canada and the United States.

Hundreds of pioneers passed through the Whitman Mission bringing a disease that affected Indians who were never exposed before. Cayuse Indians dropped like flies. Whitman warned them, but they bathed in cold water to combat the high fever and died as a result. Angered by the epidemic, the stricken Indians knew that the dreaded measles came from Whitman's Mission.

The sick were being attended at the Whitman Mission on November 29, 1847. Without warning, a Cayuse War-Party ambushed, massacred Reverend and Mrs. Whitman, eleven others, and left two others to die. Dozens of women and children were taken hostage. Thirteen people escaped into the woods, making their way to Fort Vancouver; some reached Lapwai Mission. The Cayuse War began.

During the massacre, the Nez Perce took Mrs. Spalding and her children to a safe-house, home of Indian Agent, William Craig, the first white settler in Idaho; they respected Craig, married to a Nez Perce. He abandoned his horse and fled with the help of Nez Perce women.

Nebraska Historical marker was for Narcissa Whitman, wife of Dr. Marcus missionaries came west to Christianize the Indians. The two were martyred in a Cayuse Indian massacre of the Whitman Mission. The Cayuse Indian War began, (Courtesy of Ned Eddins)

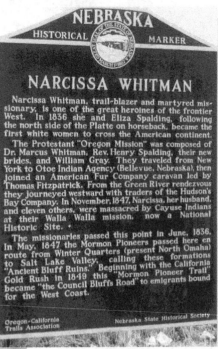

NEBRASKA HISTORICAL MARKER

NARCISSA WHITMAN

Narcissa Whitman, trail-blazer and martyred missionary, is one of the great heroines of the frontier West. In 1836 she and Eliza Spalding, following the north side of the Platte on horseback, became the first white women to cross the American continent.

The Protestant "Oregon Mission" was composed of Dr. Marcus Whitman, Rev. Henry Spalding, their new brides, and William Gray. They traveled from New York to Otoe Indian Agency (Bellevue, Nebraska), then joined an American Fur Company caravan led by Thomas Fitzpatrick. From the Green River rendezvous they journeyed westward with traders of the Hudson's Bay Company. In November, 1847, Narcissa, her husband, and eleven others, were massacred by Cayuse Indians at their Walla Walla mission, now a National Historic Site. •

The missionaries passed this point in June, 1836. In May, 1847 the Mormon Pioneers passed here en route from Winter Quarters (present North Omaha) to Salt Lake Valley, calling these formations "Ancient Bluff Ruins." Beginning with the California Gold Rush in 1849 this "Mormon Pioneer Trail" became "the Council Bluffs Road" to emigrants bound for the West Coast.

Oregon-California Trails Association   Nebraska State Historical Society

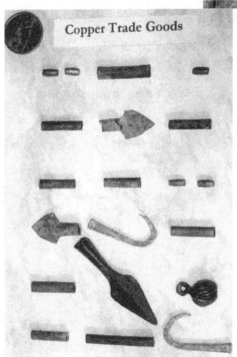

Copper Trade Goods

Copper Trade Goods-.The Hudson's BayCompany brought all kinds of goods from England for the trade arrowheads, beads, blankets, cloth, guns, gunpowder, horses, kettles, knives, pipes, tobacco, traps, and other trade goods that could be bought or bartered for furs. Author photo

When the survivors reached Fort Vancouver, chief factor McLoughlin sent Peter Skene Ogden to represent him. Ogden traded 50 blankets, 50 shirts, some handkerchiefs, tobacco, guns and ammunition for the white captives' freedom. He brought 37 captives back to Fort Vancouver with him in 1848. Five leaders of the massacre were caught (October, 1849), tried and hanged in Oregon City, in 1850. The Cayuse War ended. The missions were closed down.

As the emigrants arrived at Fort Vancouver broke, and exhausted, coming off the Oregon Trail, Chief factor, John McLoughlin gave them a house, firewood, salmon, potatoes, seed and other supplies. He resigned to found Oregon City. John is called "the Father of Oregon."

Fur trapper, Joseph Meek and party started on horse-back for Washington D.C. to seek protection from the Indians in Oregon Territory. They rode along the Oregon Trail to Fort Boise, Fort Hall and Bear River Station and traveled on snowshoes to Fort Laramie. Several dropped out. On horseback, Meek continued back East alone to meet with President Polk, his trip a success.

Polk appointed a Governor to Oregon Territory and assigned two military companies to Fort Vancouver, on March 2, 1849 and the U.S. Fourth Infantry Regiment was assigned to the Northwest for duty.

In 1863 a large sum of money was paid by the United States government to the Hudson's Bay Company for the Province of Oregon. In 1868 Britain relinquished rights to the monopoly over Rupert's Land. The Hudson's Bay Company was the first business venture in the Pacific Northwest. Hudson's Bay Company was the only kind of rule in the beginning, but laid the foundation for the U.S. Government to step in.

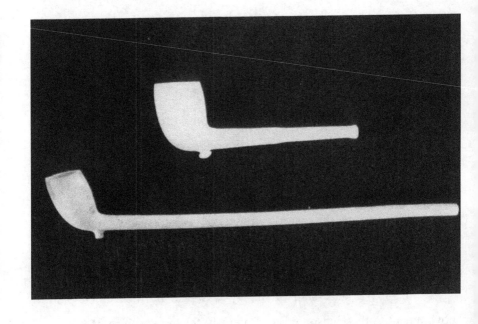

Indian Trade pipes were traded to the Native American Indians for furs. The two kaolin trade pipes were made of a fine, gray, white or yellow clay. Indians smoked a tobacco leaf indigenous to America. (Author's personal collection)

Chapter Four
Indian Trade

Long before the white man coastal Indians devised a monetary system called wampum. A mussel shell was broken into pieces by a stone hammer and each piece was rounded by abrasion. A hole was drilled in the center with a bow-drill and these were put on a leather thong to be worn around the neck. Wampum was exchanged in trade, similar to a monetary system. The Indians had established a value for a bead strand early on and they called the strands bead money.

The American Fur Trade 1670-1870 with the Native American Indian proved to be an extravagant undertaking. In the past Native Americans had made beads of bone, horn, shell, stone and wood for thousands of years. But, when white explorers introduced glass beads they quickly became popular among the Indians.

Early explorers, the Hudson's Bay Company and Fur Traders all brought glass beads to the Indians and they readily accepted them. Lewis and Clark first sat down on a blanket to trade with the Nez Perce. The Nez Perce told them they did not want red beads, but preferred blue ones. They called the pale blue donut shaped bead of the Spanish "a piece of the sky." They had obtained the precious blue Padre beads from the Spanish explorers, early on. The explorers, Lewis and Clark heard blue Padres called "tia commoshack," in the Nez Perce tongue, or chief beads.

Sky-blue glass Padre Beads were produced in China in the 1700's and 1800's. The blue bead was wound bead made by the Chinese and traded. Chinese junks met with Spanish Galleons in harbors with an interpreter to barter the precious beads. When the Spanish Galleons left Spain for the new world, they were laden with the blue beads. The name,

The Red Fox- The cunning, sly fox is a carnivorous mammal, a wild dog. The red fox was a good source of fur for the Hudsons Bay Company. Fox fur was sewn together to make elegant fur coats and hats in England   (Photo Courtesy of Ned Eddins)

Padre, came from the Spanish Catholic priests who gave the blue beads to the Southwestern Indians as prayer beads. The Padre probably was the most acclaimed trade-bead in America for the Indians.

Bone, hair-pipe and shell were used in the fur trade with the Indians. Ships brought cowry shell, dentillium and marine hair-pipe from England. Barrel, conical, discoidal, flat, ovate, rectangular, round, spherical, truncate, and tubular shell was shipped in for the fur trade. Shell was cut and drilled for wampum beads. Other materials arrived, such as copper, gold and silver.

Beads have always been a trade item to the American Indians. Vikings, Christopher Columbus, Spanish Conquistadors, and Lewis and Clark all initiated glass beads to the Indians. Beads were bartered by Fur Traders, Mountain Men and the Hudson's Bay Company to the Indians for furs. Beads were a lucrative item of trade. Indians would bring furs in trade for beads and other articles of trade. Beads, made in Bohemia, China, Czechoslovakia, England, France, Germany, Holland, Italy and Spain were bartered to the Indians by the Hudson's Bay Company.

As the fur trade unfolded many items were traded to the Indian. Blankets, guns, horses, trinkets, utensils and hundreds of other items were exchanged for furs. But one item remained the mainstay in trade - the trade bead. The Indians' fascination with the bright colored glass beads from Europe never ended. During the Fur Trade Era the Hudson's Bay Company traded thousands of glass beads to the American Indians. Beads were considered animate. They loved their bead adornment.

Tiny cut-beads beads from France were bartered, called seed beads. The seed bead was the tiniest bead traded and the Indians claimed that only a hair from the tail of a horse could penetrate the tiny hole.

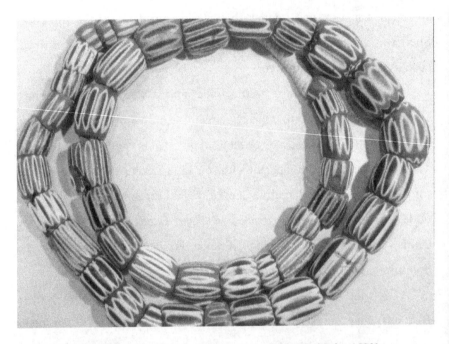

Seven Layer Venetian Chevron trade beads made in the 1500's
and used in the Fur Trade Era to barter for furs from the Indians.
Beautiful red, white and blue layered beads made in Murano,
Italy.   Courtesy of Jerry Fackrell, Crafter's Choice.

Seed beads decorated garments and moccasins. A slightly larger bead was the pound bead. It is a donut shaped bead over twice the size of a seed bead. These beads were sold in the pound increment by the bag. The colored glass beads from Europe were coveted by the Indians. Beads of every size and color were traded to them.

A slightly larger bead was the pound bead. It is a donut shaped bead twice the size of a seed bead. These beads were sold in the pound increment by the bag. The colored glass beads from Europe were coveted by the Indians. Beads of every size and color were traded to them.

A popular bead traded was called the pony bead, which was donut shaped. The size of a pony bead was just a little larger than the pound bead. Two stories are told to explain the name, "pony bead." The first story is almost a folk tale. During the fur trade with the Indians a strand of small beads eight feet in length was traded for a small pony, thus, the name pony bead. The second story arose in the way that Russian merchants used small horses to transport their bead stock across the Bering Straits. We have another clue for the name, pony bead.

A donut shaped bead than twice the size and thickness of the pony bead was the favorite of the Crow Indians. This trade bead was named for the Crow Indians. To this day the beads are called "Crow beads."

Other favorite trade beads were the "Chevron Beads." Chevrons were an attractive and unusually striped bead with a star pattern on each end. Russian blues, greenhearts, red and white hearts, blue and white hearts, yellow hearts and yellow jackets were all popular at the time.

The major producer of glass beads during the Fur Trade Era 1670-1870, was Venice, Italy. The beads were made on the island of Murano, Italy. Methods of glass manufacture were held secret by the

Padre beads- Lewis and Clark sat down on a blanket to trade with the Nez Perce. The Nez Perce did not want red beads, but blue ones, instead. They called the pale blue donut shaped bead of the Spanish explorers, "a piece of the sky."   (Author photo)

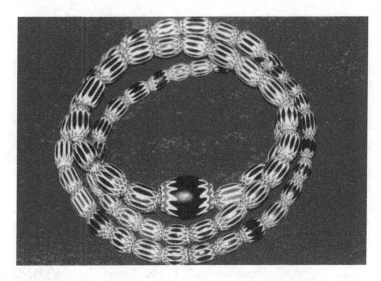

Hudson's Bay Company American Flag beads were gorgeous red, white and blue chevron glass trade beads bartered to the Indians for furs. They were gorgeous caned beads.   (Author photo)

merchant families of the Republic. Laws were passed in Venice to prevent artists from taking their trade to other countries. It became a life and death matter to keep bead technology in Italy. Their glass beads were unmatched in quality. Venetian beads shipped around the world in wooden barrels and casks represented a major portion of Italian wealth.

The beautiful Chevron bead was called Paternosters or "Father of all Beads." A gorgeous red, white, and blue bead, it is a work of art and its size gave it distinction over all other beads. Chevrons were manufactured in Murano, Italy from glass cane that had a distinctive star pattern after the Fifteenth Century. These unusual beads were made with a blow pipe gathering glass and pressing it into a tapered mold. The side had pleats to score the layers and create a star pattern. The glass gathered was then caned. The molten glass was drawn by pulling the glass for several yards before cooling it off.

It was broken off into canes and from the canes beads were cut into beads, ground on the ends and polished. The beads ranged from 3/8" to 2 1/2" long. Some chevrons were made of rich blacks, blues, greens, reds and whites. The chevron ends bore the star design. Using many steps, the result was the egg shaped bead.

Other Chevrons were green with black, brown and white. The Yellow-Jacket Chevron, like the wasp, was black and yellow, with red and white with a star pattern on the ends.

Hudson's Bay beads were traded around the Pacific Northwest. Indians liked the Cornaline d'Aleppo bead made in the 1700's in Aleppo, Italy, an export city. The Greenheart had a translucent green center, reddish brown outer layer and a clear coating on the outside. A yellow centered bead was referred to as the Yellow heart. The Greenheart was

Venetian Feather beads were mid-1800's glass beads traded for furs to the American Indians. They were lamp wound and combed to get the unusual design. They are ellipsoid and were fashioned in Murano, Italy.   Author photo

the forerunner of the White heart. The White heart had an opaque white center with a bright red outer layer.

Bohemian and Czechoslovakian beads traded to the Russians were known as Russian Blues. These beads were cobalt blue and faceted or occasionally coned and not faceted. Russian Blues were transported over the Bering Straits.

Bead making methods included the drawing technique over heat. Hollow canes were broken at correct lengths and reintroduced to heat to produce tube and round beads. Some were reheated into hex-shaped or placed in molds. Other shapes were barrel, donut, faceted, hex, round, and tubular (tube or bugle beads). Wire mandrel-wound, molded, mandrel-pressed, and blown glass beads were made.

The story of the purchase of Manhattan Island for $24.00 worth of beads is remembered in American History. Peter Stuyvesant traded red, white and blue striped Amsterdam manufactured beads for the Island of Manhattan in New York from the Indians. Actually, there were more items in the trade besides beads, but it makes a real good story!

Christopher Carson was loved by the Ute people, who
called him Father Kit. He was an explorer, farmer,
fur trapper, guide, officer, and famous Indian fighter,
Kit attained the rank of brigadier general in the U.S. Army.
(Photo Courtesy of the Idaho State Historical Society)

Chapter Five
Mountain Men

Companies from America, England, France, Russia and Spain engaged in the Fur trade. Individual mountain men like Jim Bridger and Kit Carson were fur traders. Mountain men like John Colter and George Drouillard were fur trapping legends by the time that they joined the Manuel Lisa party with the St. Louis Missouri Fur Trade Company of 1809-10. At the Three Forks of the Missouri in the spring of 1810, they assisted building "Henry's Fort" on Henry's Fork on the north fork of the Snake River in Idaho Territory.

Born in 1804 in Richmond, Virginia, young Jim Bridger took a job as apprentice to a blacksmith in St. Louis, Missouri. He left that position to sojourn down the Missouri River by keel boat, embarking on a hunting expedition under William H. Ashley, at the age eighteen. When he was twenty, Bridger made a name for himself as an explorer, discovering the Great Salt Lake. He also discovered the Bridger Mountains, Bridger Pass, and Bridger Creek and also blazed Bridger Trail. A ferry crossing and a road were all named for Bridger.

Bridger lived among the Indians and took three Native American wives. He first married a Flathead squaw, who bore him three children. Jim then married a Ute Indian woman and took a third wife, as was Indian fashion. She was the daughter of Chief Washakie of the Green and Wind River Goshute Shoshoni in Wyoming Territory. She gave birth to two children. A daughter was a student at the Whitman Mission School in Oregon. Washakie was chief over several hundred Goshiute Shoshonis. A peaceable Shoshoni, Washakie cooperated with the white man. He is credited for taking 6 enemy scalps, as coup.

Jim Bridger Memorial-Jim Bridger was a famous mountain man. He discovered the Great Salt Lake. He was a fur trapper and Indian fighter Bridger lived among the Indians and took three Native American wives in Indian fashion.
Photo Courtesy of the Idaho State Historical Society

Chief Washakie was the head of a large village of the Green and Wind River Goshiute Shoshonis in Wyoming Territory. Jim Bridger married the daughter of the Shoshoni Chief Washakie.

(Courtesy A.P.)

The Indian fighter, Jim Bridger, fought the Arikara and the Blackfeet, who were fierce foes. Bridger spoke Bannock, Shoshoni and other Indian dialects, besides the Indian sign language. He also spoke some French and Spanish.

Jim, with four partners bought out the Rocky Mountain Fur Company in 1830, a successful venture. After trapping beaver for two decades Jim Bridger and a partner, Louis Vasquez built "Fort Bridger." Built on Black's Fork of the Green River in early Wyoming (1843), Fort Bridger became a major way station along the Oregon Trail. They traded furs with the Indians, mountain men and sold to the immigrants that took the trail. In his lifetime Jim Bridger had been guide for the U.S. Army, the Union Pacific Railroad and the Overland Stage Company. He had problems with the Mormons in Salt Lake City but eventually sold them his fort. Bridger and Carson were trapping partners in the old days.

A legendary story was told about Jim Bridger. A small band of angry Blackfeet Indians was in hot pursuit of Bridger. They disliked him trapping animals in their territory. His horse became lathered as he rode for his life, as he retreated, his horse in a full gallop, headed for his fort. Jim managed to stay alive, kept his scalp, but caught an arrow in the back. He survived for three years with the arrow-head in his backbone. Finally, a physician removed it without anesthetic.

Captain Bonneville, on army leave in 1832 trapped for beaver. In 1833, Bonneville noted several large herds of buffalo near Pocatello.

Jedediah Strong Smith (1798-1831) was one of the most popular mountain men of the Fur Trade era. He was known in western history, as an adventurer and explorer. Smith was a colorful character, who always carried a Bible and a Hawken rifle. Smith and his two partners sold the

69

Rocky Mountain Fur Company in 1830. Having become rich, he bought a mansion in St. Louis, which included slaves.

In 1823, Jedediah had a run in with a bear. The grizzly attacked Smith's horse from the rear, clawing both him and his horse. The frightened steed dragged the snarling bruin, teeth and claws engaged, nearly 150 feet before kicking and pulling free. Smith's scalp on the left side, eyebrow and ear were torn loose. The skin was crudely sewn back on. From then on he parted his hair to hide the scars. Jedediah narrowly escaped death from the bear.

Just eight years later he headed up a trading expedition on the Santa Fe Trail. While seeking water for the group, Smith encountered a war party of Comanche Indians. Although he killed their chief, he was either captured or killed and never seen again.

Christopher Houston Carson was born in 1809. His parents said that he was no bigger than a "kit" beaver at birth, and was nicknamed, Kit. He would become one of America's most famous mountain men and Indian fighters. Kit was raised in Missouri and worked as an apprentice to a saddle maker. Fleeing the apprenticeship bond Kit signed up on a caravan to Santa Fe, herding livestock. Carson went from there to Taos, where he made his permanent home. Carson trapped for furs in the Rockies for years, trapping with men like Jim Bridger, Thomas Fitzpatrick, and Joe Meek. Kit trapped for the Hudson's Bay Company.

Carson lived around the Indians, learning customs and languages. Kit fought them on dozens of occasions and was a good Indian fighter. He fought Arapaho, Blackfeet, Comanche, Kiowa, and Navajo Indians. At the Rendevouz of 1835 on Green River, Kit Carson fought in a life-or-death duel with a French mountain man, named Shunar, over a young

Shoshoni Country in Wyoming Territory and also the stomping grounds of famed mountain man, Jim Bridger, married to the chief's daughter. (Courtesy N.E.)

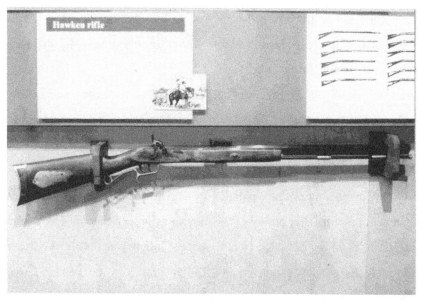

The Hawkin rifle made famous by Jedediah Strong Smith, one of the most famous mountain men. Smith always carried a bible and a Hawken rifle. (Courtesy Three Island Crossing State Park)

Arapaho Indian woman, named Waanike. They rode toward each other with pistols drawn. Kit shot Shunar, but let him live, when he begged for mercy. Kit won the duel and married Waanike. She bore him two children, but died young. His second wife was a Cheyenne Indian squaw.

Kit teamed up on a fur trade expedition in 1838. The company trapped furs in Navajo land. Carson worked for a time as a scout into Apache country and farmed in New Mexico with Lucien Maxwell.

Carson first served in the U.S. Army as a scout for the "Pathfinder," Lieutenant John Charles Freemont. He also scouted for Lieutenant Freemont on a trek from the Great Salt Lake in Utah into Oregon in 1842 along the Oregon Trail. The purpose of the expedition was the American acquisition of the state of Oregon.

In 1843 Carson returned to his beloved Taos and became an Indian agent for the Ute Indians, who referred to him as "Father Kit." It was here that Kit met and married Josefa Jaramillo, his third wife, in 1843. Josefa and Kit had seven children.

Kit served under Freemont in his California Battalion and briefly in the Bear Flag Republic. In 1846 Carson fought at San Pasqual and at the battle of San Gabriel River in California during the Mexican War. His biography was written in 1858.

Carson joined the Union Army and fought in the Civil War as lieutenant colonel, later attaining the rank of brigadier general. He led the brigade of the First New Mexico Volunteer Infantry at the Battle of the Adobe Walls in 1864 against 3,000 Indian braves in the Panhandle of Texas. Twenty five years after Kit wed Josefa, she died; Kit mourned her and in poor health died one month later; Kit and Josefa were interred side by side.

Chapter Six
Wagons West

After 1842, American emigrants embarked in vast numbers on the long 2,000 mile journey West by covered wagon in trains from St. Louis on the Oregon Trail bound for Oregon. Wagons were formed in a circle at night, called a corral with guards posted to ward off danger. There was safety in numbers. A vote determined a train captain and other officers. Guides were employed to lead the wagons westward. Pioneer wagons lined the Oregon Trail for miles.

As pioneers forged westward, they followed many of the routes carved out buy early explorers. The McKenzie Hunt Trail led from Missouri to Astoria, in Oregon Territory. The ever popular Mormon and Oregon Trail became main routes traveled by thousands.

Marcus Whitman headed up a massive wagon-train into Oregon in 1843. Thousands of emigrants followed. Emigrant wagon trains dotted the horizon. As American settlers traveled west by wagon train, they came under Indian attack. The President of the United States ordered the U.S. Calvary to the western front to protect the emigrant wagon trains, miners and settlers from Indian attacks.

Euro-Americans all headed west from St. Louis along the Oregon Trail to their destinations in California and Oregon Territories. Women and children often traveled in wagons. Others rode horse or mules. Some simply walked along the wagons. There was a great movement as people pushed westward.

There were two types of covered wagons. The heavier Conestoga wagon was manufactured first. The Conestoga had broader wheels than the Prairie Schooner and was more heavily constructed. The Prairie

73

View of the Scottsbluff region and Chimney Rock from the Oregon Trail were photographed in western Nebraska. The rock formations outside of Scottsbluff, Nebraska are important landmarks, today.   (Courtesy N.E.)

Scenes from the old Oregon Trail- Top view is of the City of Rocks in eastern Idaho (Courtesy N.E.) bottom view of Lizard Butte, outside of Marsing, Idaho on the Snake River on the South Alternate route of the Oregon Trail.   (Author photo)

Schooner weighed just one ton. It outlived the Conestoga. Prairie Schooners were compared to sailing ships, moving on the ocean.

A common site along the Oregon Trail was oxen pulling a covered wagon. To see oxen is a rare site, today. Draft animals, horses, mules and oxen were used to pull the wagons. But horses were too expensive for the job. Oxen sold for less money, pulled more weight, remained stationery at night, and their meat was more edible.

On a good day, a covered wagon pulled by oxen could cover 20 miles, banning slowdowns, but days had slow-downs. Two oxen pulled the Prairie Schooner with two yokes. Freighters were heavier and employed four oxen. Heat exhaustion killed many mules and oxen on the trail.

The pioneers faced hardship and danger on their trek west. Bandits, disease, extreme temperatures, flooded river crossings, Indians, rattlesnakes, rough terrain, and wild animals faced them on their journey. Swarms of mosquitoes could plague the animals and humans in swamp land. Thousands of pioneers died on the trail.

Roads back then were crude over rough terrain. At first many roads were non-existent and had to be forged. Others began as migratory animal paths that had become Indian hunting trails. Wagons blazed trails leaving ruts that are still seen today along the old Oregon Trail.

Many wagons were left abandoned and often pieces of furniture were removed from wagons to lighten the emigrant's load. Furniture littering the Oregon Trail became a familiar sight to westward travelers.

The Three Island Crossing was a very famous Snake River site to cross the Snake River at the junction of the Oregon Trail and site for the ferry. Besides being a major river crossing, drinking water was potable. Thousands of pioneers passed this way.

Conestoga Wagon   at Three Island Crossing State Park -The Conestoga wagon was the original mode of transportation used to carry the emigrant, his family and goods westward on the Oregon Trail. Some wagon ruts still remain in the background across the river on the down slope of the old Oregon Trail.

(Author photo)

The gentleman that owned the ferry was Gus Glenn. The town of Glenn's Ferry was named after him. The present day Three Island Crossing State Park outside Glenn's Ferry along the Snake River has a museum, wagons and a good view of the trail descent to the river. The ruts can be seen on the down slope of the far bank of the Snake River and the three islands they crossed, today.

If the wagons continued along the south side of the Snake they took the southern route, which was more rugged and a tougher trip. If the river was crossed, the northern route west was taken. The two trails would not intersect again until reaching old Fort Boise.

In August members of the town of Glenn's Ferry, Idaho conduct a yearly reenactment of the difficult crossing that faced pioneers wanting to ford or ferry across the Snake River there in the mid 1800s. Oxen and horse teams pull several covered wagons across the river, aided by many men on horseback.

There were two types of covered wagons. The Conestoga wagon was manufactured first and the Prairie Schooner came later. The Conestoga wagon was more heavily constructed and had broader wheels. The Prairie Schooner was lighter weighing just one ton and it outlived the Conestoga. The lighter Prairie Schooners were compared to sailing ships, moving on the ocean.

Horses, mules and oxen were used to pull the emigrant wagons. Oxen were much stronger animals and made better time. Two or four oxen pulled the Prairie Schooner with two or four yokes. Freighters were heavier, using two oxen. Exhaustion killed many mules and oxen on the trail due to extreme heat.

In 1842 Conestoga wagons began leaving St. Louis, Missouri for Oregon Territory on the Oregon Trail. Emigrants traveled in wagon-trains, to gain protection from marauding Indians and horse thieves.   (Author photo)

Wyoming shrines lie along the Oregon Trail where the California, Mormon and Oregon Trails crossed the Continental Divide at 7546 feet in elevation on the South end of the Wind River Mountains   (Courtesy N.E.)

Hundreds of wagons could be seen, people riding mules, riding horseback or just walking headed west from St. Louis along the Oregon Trail. There was a great movement as people pushed westward.

Routes forged out by early explorers led westward. The McKenzie-Hunt trail led from Missouri to Astoria, Oregon. The ever popular Oregon Trail and Mormon Trail became main routes traveled by thousands.

Major cattle trails were utilized by cattlemen to drive their herds west. Cattle trails from Kansas City to Abilene, St. Louis and Omaha were forged and Cow towns emerged. Chuck-wagons were built to meet the needs of a drover on the cattle trail.

Chuck-wagons had a toolbox on one side, a water barrel on the other and a chuck-box in back. The wagon contained drawers and shelves to hold dishes, food, other provisions, and a work table for the cook. Underneath the chuck-box lay the boot that held ovens and skillets. The wagon bed held bedrolls, lanterns, guns, ammo, spare wheel, etc.

A real need for a military fort became apparent as Indians constantly raided wagon trains and stage lines. The army planned to build a centrally located military garrison in the Boise Valley.

A wagon-train headed west for Fort Boise along the Oregon Trail, in August 1854. The Ward party of 23 people decided to have a picnic on the Boise River, just south of president day Middleton, Idaho.

They had unhitched their wagons, when older brother, Robert ran in shouting, "the Indians have stolen a horse." Hitching up their horses, the Ward party pulled their rigs onto the road, trying to escape; but they became surrounded by 200 renegade Snake Indians. Alexander Ward, their leader was shot and killed instantly. Arrows and bullets flew, as all hell broke loose. By sunset, all adult males in the party had perished.

79

The Ward Massacre Monument lies south of the Boise River and Middleton, Idaho. A marker stands in memory of the Ward family. They left the wagon train, on August 20, 1854 to have a picnic but were massacred by savages. *(Author photo)*

Markers exist along the old Oregon Trail today. It is estimated that hundreds of thousands of pioneers crossed on the Oregon Trail after the Whitmans made the first journey. Thousands of people died on that rugged trek. *(Author and N.E. photo)*

Renegades attacked the wagons, women and children, stripping Mrs. Ward and her teen-age daughter naked. Possibly raped, the Ward women were slashed to ribbons with knives; their flesh seared with firebrands. Mrs. Ward was brutally bludgeoned to death and her 17 year old daughter died, during horrific torture. Screaming in pain and horror, three little girls were burned alive.

Three other children just disappeared. The savages burned the wagons and fled The teen-age boys, both struck by arrows, crawled into the brush during the attack saving their lives. William, showing much bravery, walked miles to Fort Boise, an arrow through his lung. Newton was later found alive.

At Fort Dalles, Oregon Major Rains ordered Haller and 26 soldiers to pursue the renegades. 39 volunteers, under Nathan Olney, with some Nez Perce and Umatillas volunteered to ride behind the U.S. Cavalry. Arriving at the massacre site Haller buried 18 bodies. Haller found the renegade's trail into the coming. Later they caught and lynched some of the attackers. General John Wool ordered Haller and 150 men back to the Ward Massacre Site in the spring of 1855. Haller took Nathan Olney, Indian agent, with him.

Gallows were built, with nooses. Wagons were rolled out from under them. They were hanged and cut them down for burial the next morning. Haller rode with his detachment down the Boise, Payette and Snake Rivers, flushing out any of Ward's attackers to be hanged on the spot. Eighteen were hanged, the exact number killed in the massacre.

The Ward Massacre Memorial stands on the old Oregon Trail as a monument of the massacre of the Ward family wagon-train just south of present day Middleton, Idaho (August 20, 1854).

Lerry Heath completes his Snake River crossing during Glenn's Ferry's Three Island Crossing Reenactment Days, driving wagon and oxen. Oxen are a rare sight in America, today. The reenactment is very realistic.   (Photo courtesy of Lerry Heath)

1855-1878 was a time of Indian uprisings. Snake Indians in eastern Idaho were raising havoc with wagon-trains passing through along the Oregon Trail. The slow moving processions were easy targets for marauding Indians. Massacres or skirmishes occurred on a daily basis. Renegades attacked the wagon-trains traveling through eastern Idaho Territory. The Indian skirmishes continued.

The Ward Party Massacre, in 1854 was followed by the Modoc Indian rebellion in Oregon Territory in 1855. In Washington Territory there was an active military campaign against the Yakima Indians in 1856. The Palouse Indians in northern Idaho executed raids in 1858.

Eighteen year old Starr Wilkinson was a 6 foot 8 inch, 300 pound half-breed. Having a Cherokee Indian-negro mother and a white father, Wilkinson began his trip west around 1856, from St. Louis by wagon-train. He loved a girl, named Jesse Smith, who jilted him for another man. Her new lover was a Mr. York.

Wilkinson caught the couple lying in the sagebrush, near the Snake River. He drowned the man in the river as they fought and later jumped from the train. While on the run Wilkinson met a group of Paiute Indians and joined their band. They called him Nampa, in Paiute or "Bigfoot."

He would later become their leader. It was reported that he also teamed up with Joe Lewis, a notorious French Canadian. In the meantime the wagon-train returned to St. Louis, due to harsh winter. When the wagon-train returned, Nampa and his Paiute band massacred all of the passengers (including his ex-girlfriend) and burned the wagons.

He led the renegades on stagecoach raids, along Reynolds Creek, on the Boise-Silver City road. On these raids the man (who never rode a horse) soon to be known as Bigfoot ran along a moving stage. He whooped and hollered, scaring the passengers nearly to death. The outlaws became quite a nuisance robbing stages again and again, near the mining town of Silver City, Idaho.

Then the army discovered a bare 17 1/2" footprint on the Weiser River. The story of a mysterious "Bigfoot" appeared in the Idaho Statesman Newspaper in 1868 with the offer of a $1,000.00 reward for "BIGFOOT," DEAD or ALIVE.

The next time Bigfoot ran alongside the stagecoach, John Wheeler, a bounty hunter, was poised in the Aspen trees nearby with his long-rifle. He shot at Bigfoot with his 44 caliber repeating rifle. Bigfoot vanished.

Then Wheeler saw a tumble-weed moving oddly along the ground. He began firing at the weed. The hulk of a man began running wildly in Wheeler's direction. He shot Bigfoot 16 times. Wheeler apologized for shooting him, to disable the last limb. Nampa related the story of his life in exchange for an Indian burial. He died at just 30.

He became the namesake of Nampa, Idaho. The "Bigfoot" legend didn't end and rumors of Bigfoot or his ghost are yet alive in the Owyhee desert and the Northwest.

July 26, 1859, a small wagon train was attacked at Twin Springs, near Bear River. On July 27, 1859, south of Twin Springs, some shepherds were massacred. The next day Snakes raided wagons at the Hudspeth Cutoff. On August 31, 1859, Shoshonis massacred the Miltimore family in the American Falls vicinity.

From 1860-1863 the Snake Indians made a series of raids on trains in eastern Idaho Territory. On October 16, 1860 Snake renegades massacred the Utter Party west of Castle Butte in Owyhee County.

On August 9, 1862 emigrants traveled westward. The Smart wagon train was followed by the Adams, Wilson and Kennedy trains, in close proximity. One half mile from Massacre Rocks, a Snake War-party ambushed the Smart wagons and massacred the Adam's train.

They attacked and killed settlers, stole their livestock and burned their wagons, killing ten emigrants. In retaliation, California volunteers massacred a Shoshoni Indian Village near the Bear River. In 1863 Fort Boise was built. The army knew of the plight of the defenseless emigrants and the need for a fort to protect them.

The Pony express ran from St. Louis to Sacramento with riders that carried mail, from 1860-1861. About the same time, stage-lines were established that were run mostly by independents. Stage-coaches carried freight mail, passengers and payroll across western America.

Thousands of Chinese built the railroad. The transcontinental railroad was completed in 1869. The Indians called a locomotive, the "Iron Horse." Rails reached from Granger, Wyoming to Huntington, Oregon, supplied Boise by 1884. Buffalo hunters killed thousands of bison that were left to rot; the railroad hauled hides at a profit.

The steamship, "Shoshone" hauled passengers and freight between Farewell Bend and Weiser to Owyhee Crossing, 100 miles away. With few trees on the Snake River for fuel, the Shoshone was beached.

Later, the steamship was ordered to the Columbia for duty. The ship's captain had to run the ship through Hell's Canyon rapids, causing considerable damage. Fully repaired, the Shoshone ran on the Columbia River for many years.

Johnithan Keeney

Ferry master Johnithan Keeney with two partners, initiated a ferry crossing in 1863, near the Fort Boise site to ferry wagons across the Snake River for $5.00. A ferry house was built for guests and a stage line stop was added. Keeney built a trading post, in 1863 on the Malheur River. Keeney Pass was named for him. (Courtesy Idaho State Historical S

Chapter Seven
Forts on the Oregon Trail

With the threat of Indian attack forts were needed for protection or refuge. Camps, fur forts, military posts, settler's forts and stage line forts provided protection from Indians. "David Thompson's Trading Post," near East Hope (1809,) also called "Kalispell House," was the first trade fort in primitive Idaho. It consisted of three log cabins. "Fort Howse" on Clark's Fork River and "Michael Kinville's Post," at Bonner's Ferry were raised in 1810. All three were North West Company forts.

The first fort, west of the Continental Divide, was "Fort Henry," also called "Andrew Henry's Post" was built in 1810. "Skitswist Post" was a temporary post on Lake Coeur d'Alene (1812) and "Donald McKenzie's Post" was also built that year near Lewiston on the Clearwater River. Both were Pacific Fur Company forts. The next year, the North West Company bought Pacific Fur Company and the fort.

The mouth of the Boise River was fan shaped, with three channels, divided by islands. The river was four and a half feet deep and swift, flowing into the Snake, once referred to as Lewis River. Three fur forts were built by beaver hunters at the mouth of the Boise River, also called Reed's River. In 1813 John Reed built John "Reed's Post," the first Fort Boise post there. Donald McKenzie used the "Fort Boise" location as a temporary fur fort and rendezvous point in 1819. In 1834 Thomas McKay would come to the mouth of the Boise and build the third fort there, called "Fort Snake" and later named, "Old Fort Boise."

McKenzie constructed "Fort Nez Perce" along the Columbia River at the mouth of the Walla-Walla River in 1818 for the North West Company. McKenzie, a 300 pound mountain man, erected stockade walls twenty feet high, six inches thick to withstand Indian attack. The corners had bastions that housed cannons and a two hundred gallon water supply. Alexander Ross was first to run the fort.

Hudson's Bay Company purchased the North West Company in 1822 and refurbished Fort Nez Perce in 1831; it was burned to the ground and rebuilt ten years later. During the Indian wars of 1855-1856, Fort Nez Perce was abandoned and later became "Fort Walla-Walla."

Fort Laramie

The Wyoming area fur trappers opened "Fort Laramie" along the Oregon Trail in 1834, at the confluence of the Laramie and North Platte Rivers. Trade was initiated between the fur traders and the local Indians. It became a favorite stopping place for emigrant wagons bound for California. The fort was converted to an army post of good size, boasting 150 structures. Fort Laramie, now a soldier fort, protected settlers from hostile Indians and kept the peace.

There was an old cemetery on the grounds of the fort dating back to the American Fur Company and Bill Sublette, who started the fort. Fort Laramie Hospital had a 12 bed ward, dispensary, dining room and post surgeon's office. The hospital was constructed of lime grout cement.

At the Treaty of Fort Laramie Cheyenne and Sioux Chiefs, Spotted Tail, Roman Nose, Old-Man-Afraid-of-His Horses, Lone Horn, Whistling Elk, Pipe and Slow Bull all met with peace commissioners to negotiate possibly the most important peace treaty with the Indians of the 19th Century. It closed the Bozeman Trail and created the great Sioux Reservation. The Treaty of Fort Laramie, signed in 1851, with the Arapaho, Cheyenne, Crow, Sioux and other Plains tribes gave emigrants peace of mind. By 1890 the fort was closed, as Indian Wars declined.

13 year old Thomas McKay worked aboard the ship Tonquin as clerk for John Jacob Astor. They reached the Oregon coast at the mouth of the Columbia River, where Astor established "Fort Astoria." Supplies were unloaded from the Tonquin to the fort. McKay remained there for five years as clerk. He married a Chinook Indian girl, who bore him three sons. The Northwest Fur Company bought out the Astor Fur Company.

McKay and Nathaniel Wyeth were present at the Green River Rendezvous in 1834. One would build "Fort Snake," the other, "Fort Hall." McKay chose a fort location on Idaho's western border, at the site where Reed and McKenzie had their forts. Shoshonis held their Salmon fishery at the mouth of the Boise River for years. Local Shoshonis warned McKay not to build the fort there; that the river would "change its mind." This prophecy would come to haunt him.

Fort Boise, Fort Hall and Fort Laramie fur forts were erected in 1834. Fort Hall was a stockade fort built by Nathaniel Wyeth, 300 miles east of Fort Boise. Wyeth's luck was bad and he wound up selling the fur trade post to the Hudson's Bay Company. By 1856 the fort was abandoned. When Fort Hall closed, it became an Indian School serving as a schoolhouse for the Shoshoni-Paiute Indians.

In 1870 the US Cavalry built a fort south of Blackfoot. Various denominations of American Churches sent missionaries to the Indians at Fort Hall. There were Catholic, Episcopal, Mormon and Presbyterian missionaries assigned to the Indians. Episcopal missionaries built a boarding school for Indian children. A Catholic bishop initiated a cemetery for red men and white men, alike. In 1891, Miss Frost started a Presbyterian Mission School to teach Paiute and Shoshoni Indian children.

Fort Boise Drawing- In 1834, the Hudson's Bay Company welcomed trade with the Western Shoshoni and Northern Paiute Indians. The fort acted as both general store and trading post and would later add a ferry and a stage stop. The Whitman party passed through Fort Boise in 1836.
(Artist's conception by Boise artist, Len Sodenkamp)

90

In 1834 Thomas McKay built "Fort Snake," which was active until 1855. He constructed the edifice of wood. The Hudson's Bay Company bankrolled McKay and hired him as a factor, in the position of clerk. John Finley was the first Postmaster at Fort Snake. The fort was established in 1834 by the Hudson's Bay Company. It served as both general store and trading post. Furs were traded by the Shoshoni and Paiute Indians. The fort would later add a ferry and a stage stop.

The Hudson's Bay Company welcomed trade with the Western Shoshoni and Northern Paiute Indians in 1834. The fort acted as both general store and trading post and later added a ferry and a stage stop. The Whitman party passed through Fort Boise in 1836.

Hudson's Bay trappers hunted beaver in brigades, bringing their furs to Old Fort Snake, as did independents and Indians. Hudson's Bay Company appointed John McKay as chief trader to oversee trapping on the Snake River Plain for one year, but he preferred leading brigades to other duties.

Fort Snake was described as four sided, 100 feet square. The stockade sides were 14 feet high, made of logs. The entrance was on the west. The main building ran length-wise north to south. It contained a large dining area, kitchen and sleeping apartments. The stockade housed officers and servants. On the north was the store.

On the south was the servant dwelling. Behind the main building was an outdoor oven. In the northeast corner of the stockade was the bastion. Another rampart was added later, for fortification. The roof was made of split cottonwood poles, and covered with mud. There was a corral 80 feet x 90 feet. The kitchen was 10 feet' x 12 feet. The milk house measured 8 feet x 12 feet. A two story bastion stood in the north

91

east and southwest corners. There were three dwelling apartments 10 feet x 47 feet. One dwelling house was 15 feet x 45 feet. An Indian dwelling measured 10 feet x 15 feet. The stockade fort walls were 400 sq. feet. The horse corral measured 80 feet x 90 feet. It may have been used for catching horses originally. The corral was made of upright cottonwood poles lashed together and anchored, 7 feet' high. Adobe walls 11/4 feet wide were added later. The corral was suitable for cattle and horses.

The fort was described as a stockade fort with cool water, cottonwood trees, a green grassy valley, a hot spring, garden, a pasture for the horses, and Indian teepees on the landscape. Fish were plentiful here. It became an important stop along the Oregon Trail for emigrants to acquire much needed supplies and wagon trains which forded the Snake, there. It was a central location for the Indians and white man alike.

Famous explorer, John C. Fremont arrived at Fort Snake. He accurately described the fort as being on the right bank of the Snake River a mile below the mouth of the Boise River at elevation 2100 feet. Longitude 116 degrees, 47 minutes, and no seconds: Latitude 43 degrees, 48 minutes 22 seconds.

Captain Francois Payette was chosen to manage Fort Snake. Payette was a fat, jolly, enterprising Frenchman who was well liked. He brought Hawaiian natives from Fort Vancouver as servants. Fort Snake employees prided themselves on good hospitality and meals. Guests dined on salmon dinners with vegetables from his garden and drank fresh milk, provided by a cow an emigrant had abandoned. Emigrant wagons and even the stage coaches stopped at the fort; pioneers could freshen up and purchase supplies.

(1834) Wyoming Territory fur trappers established Fort Laramie on the Oregon Trail for trade with local Indians. It was converted to a soldier fort. A hospital was built. It had a 12 bed ward, dispensary, dining room and post surgeon's office. Photo courtesy of Ned Eddins.

Treaty at Fort Laramie signed in 1851, with Arapaho, Cheyenne, Crow, and Sioux tribes. (Left to right) Chiefs Spotted Tail, Roman Nose, Old-Man-Afraid-of-His Horses, Lone Horn, Whistling Elk, Pipe and Slow Bull met with agents to negotiate peace. (Photo Courtesy of Azusa Publishing, L.L.C.)

Hawaiians spoke little English and said "Hawaii," with a silent H. One heard the sounds, Owyhee, a misnomer that stuck. To this day, the arid region south of the Snake River is known as the Owyhee Desert.

The Hudson's Bay Company brought all kinds of goods from England for the trade: beads, blankets, cloth, guns, gunpowder, horses, kettles, knives, pipes, tobacco, and other trade goods that could be bartered for trinkets, utensils and lots of beads. In the fur trade six green or yellow beads traded for a beaver pelt from the Indians. The universal measure of a beaver pelt stretched and dried was a "made beaver." Each pelt was one point in trade.

The Hudson's Bay Company took advantage of the beaver fur trade east of the Rocky Mountains. Fort Boise in 1834 welcomed trade with the Western Shoshoni and Northern Paiute Indians and would trade every variety of goods in exchange for animal pelts. It acted as both general store and trading post.

Inventories from posts of the Hudson Bay Company list numerous varieties of glass, shell, and stone trade beads which were exchanged in trading post's stores. The fort would later add a ferry and a stage stop. Fort Snake became the center of the lower Snake River fur trade and an important supply stop on the Oregon Trail.

The Hudson's Bay Company welcomed trade with the emigrants, Snake Indians and mountain men along the trail. In 1835 Snake Fort profited 411 pounds. The Hudson's Bay Company acquired the Fort in 1836 with a profit of 977 pounds that year. The fort would later add a ferry and a stage stop. In 1836, Marcus Whitman's party passed through.

Francois Payette moved the Fort Boise location farther north, in the same vicinity in 1838. He added adobe mud for the outer wall around the fort fourteen feet high and three feet thick. Before long, a settlement of Shoshoni Indians camped near the fort in their teepees.

The Hudson's Bay Company renamed the fort, Fort Boise in 1839, the year the Peoria party arrived at Fort Boise. Joe Meek, William Craig and Robert Newell brought their wagons across the Blue Mountains from Fort Boise in 1840. Other famous visitors were John C. Freemont, Captain John Sutter, Marcus Whitman, Henry Spalding and their wives.

1841 and 1842 were slow years for Fort Boise. The buffalo and beaver were disappearing. 125 pioneers passed through Fort Boise, in 1842. Business picked up in 1843. In 1844 Francois Payette left the Hudson's Bay Company after twenty years service. John McLoughlin, wrote Idaho Governor George Simpson in 1845, advising him that James Craigie, a Scot, had been appointed to run Fort Boise.

Fort Boise sustained damage in 1853 from the flood waters of the Snake River overflowing its banks. The Shoshoni warning was not heeded and now the channels were shifting and eroding the fort. Severe spring flooding again washed over its banks in 1855. The flood destruction, the Ward party massacre of 1854 and the 1855 Indian Wars all contributed to closure of old Fort Boise. Employees and travelers didn't feel safe there anymore. So Fort Boise, Fort Hall and Fort Walla-Walla all closed about the same time in 1855, due to Indian uprisings.

Military Forts

In 1848 "Fort Kearney" had been established at the juncture of the Oregon Trail and the Platte River in Nebraska Territory. Fort Kearney was the first military post on the Oregon Trail. It boasted up to 2,000 emigrants and 10,000 oxen passing through in one day. The fort was a Pony Express station and later a stage line stop. And in 1849, Peg-Leg Smith established Fort Smith on the Oregon Trail, near Montpelier.

(1855) Fort Lemhi became a Mormon fort stockade, with 25 cabins and an adobe corral. Indian attacks closed this fort in 1858. Lewis and Clark camped there after crossing Lemhi Pass in 1805. At the site, "Camp Boise River" was again established by the army in 1855, at old Fort Boise. It was maintained for just six weeks and abandoned in 1862, when the Snake River of swept Fort Boise away

Old Fort Boise was located five miles northwest of the present day Parma, Idaho (named for Parma, Italy). A replica of Fort Boise was constructed in Parma, Idaho; it contains a park, cabin and museum.

Jonathon Keeney, who had come across on the Oregon Trail, himself was now a merchant from Placerville. He initiated a ferry crossing in 1863, near the Fort Boise site to accommodate passengers wanting to ford the Snake River. This was a popular crossing for the local Indians, emigrants and fur traders that passed Fort Boise. Keeney and two partners, Duval and McLaughlin established the ferry service.

They charged $5.00 as an average to ferry a wagon across the river. Shipments from Boise Basin mining towns provided revenue for Keeney. The ferry site became a stage line stop. A ferry house was built for the guests. Keeney established a trading post in 1863 on the Malheur River. Keeney Pass on the Oregon Trail was named after him.

Pinkney Lugenbeel was born on November 16, 1816 in Liberty, Maryland. He graduated from West Point in 1840. Lugenbeel served in many American forts, gaining experience. He served on frontier duty and through the Mexican War and attained the rank of captain in 1855.

Fort Hall Drawing- Fort Hall was built in 1834. It was a stockade fort built by Nathaniel Wyeth 300 miles east of Fort Boise. Fort Boise and Fort Hall competed for the fur trade business. Wyeth finally sold his fur trade post to the Hudson's Bay Company. By 1856 the fort was abandoned.

(Artist's conception by Boise artist, Len Sodenkamp)

Lugenbeel was assigned to Fort Vancouver, Washington Territory. The captain fought in the Yakima Indian Wars in 1856. He was stationed at Fort Dalles in Oregon Territory from 1856-1859 and in Colville, Washington Territory 1859-1861. He was promoted through the ranks. Major Lugenbeel was in command at Fort Vancouver when the Civil War broke out. He trained recruits, there from 1861-1863, when he was ordered to establish a fort in the Boise Basin to protect the citizenry.

In 1863 Major Lugenbeel was ordered by the War Department to establish a fort in Idaho Territory, an extension of Fort Vancouver. He headed up the 9th Infantry, with Companies D, F, G & H, 1st Washington Territory Infantry, and one detachment of the 1st Oregon Cavalry from Fort Vancouver, en route to the Boise Basin.

During the Civil War the Battle of Gettysburg was fought on July 3, 1863. The next day on July 4, 1863 Cyrus Jacobs, H.C. Riggs, John Hailey, Frank and Tom Davis from Idaho City met with Major Lugenbeel on a site where only jack-rabbits, rattle-snakes, sagebrush, some log cabins and a distant farm existed.

Since the Indian Wars of 1855, the need for a military outpost in the area was great. A spot at the foot of the Rockies, along the Oregon Trail where the Owyhee Desert meets the foothills, near a stream on firm ground in the Boise River Valley was picked by Major Lugenbeel. Cottonwood Creek skirted the camp and flowed into the Boise River and teemed with salmon. He named the site, "Camp Boise River" at the junction of the roads to Silver City and Idaho City crossed, as the Gold Rush began. The fort was to protect the miners, settlers and emigrants, along the Oregon Trail. Indians called it a "soldier fort," apart from the Hudson's Bay Company. The fort was later named "Fort Boise."

The old Fort Boise Replica Museum inside the town of Parma, Idaho is located 5 miles southeast of the original fort at the mouth of the Boise, River and the Snake River. The facsimile was built exactly 100' x 100', with bastions on opposing corners. Inside is a historical museum.

(Courtesy of the Fort Boise Replica Museum)

Tom Davis chose fertile ground, south of the Boise River, for a farm. His choice was near the old "Emigrant Crossing," where emigrants had forded the Boise River. The founding fathers chose the four mile land strip in between the two picks for the future Boise City and platted the township between the fort site and the river.

Major Lugenbeel was the overseer of the initial phase of Fort Boise with a saw mill driven by mules, a limestone kiln, adobe yard, and a sandstone quarry at Table Rock Mesa. Major Lugenbeel built army barracks to house five companies of U.S. Cavalry. Officer's quarters of hewn sandstone were constructed along Officer's Row, a street that still exists. Jobs were subcontracted for hay, stored on islands on the Boise River and shingles were used in construction for roofing. Cottonwood logs were used for cabins and split in two for roofing. These could be covered with adobe mud or bricks for insulation and protection.

Three buildings from the original fort are still standing. Building #1 was an officer's barracks on Officer's Row. The old barracks served as a doctor's residence for a time. Recently the Veteran's Administration used this building for Human Resource Services but is now the Regional Counsel & Employee Education Services building. Building #4 on Officer's Row, built in 1870 as part of Fort Boise was originally used as officers' quarters. Walls were insulated. U.S. Cavalry Officers were housed here to defend the local citizenry from Indian uprising. Now deserted, there is rumor that this old relic is haunted. Building #6, built in 1863 as part of Fort Boise, was originally used as the Quartermaster Building headquarters.

These two barracks and the quartermaster building were made of hewn sandstone blocks, some weighing 25-1,000 pounds each, quarried

West Point graduate Major Pinkney Lugenbeel received an assignment in 1863 regarding the Indian attacks and a need to protect the citizens in Idaho Territory. He was ordered to leave Fort Vancouver with five companies of U.S. Cavalry and Infantry for the Boise Basin.

(Courtesy Idaho State Historical Library)

at Table Rock, east of Boise, Idaho, by the Oregon Volunteers. They were insulated with rock rubble and adobe. The Quartermaster Building was the first insulated building in Boise City in 1863 and is currently a medical facility used as the Eye Clinic. All three buildings are still standing. The plaques on the old structures were provided by the Veterans Administration Bicentennial Memorial on July 4, 1976.

The old Fort Boise stone guard-house stood at the entrance to Fort Boise. A guard was posted around the clock. Anyone entering Fort Boise had to pass through this gate. All civilians, soldiers, and vendors papers were checked at the guard station before entering. A bronze plaque was placed on the guard house at the entrance to Fort Boise, in north residential Boise, Idaho.

The enlisted men were likely housed in log barracks. A stockade was built to house deserters, the drunk and disorderly. A blacksmith shop and bake shop were constructed. Log quarters were erected for the women who worked in the laundry. Dr. Fitzgerald was the first army doctor assigned to the fort. A school was established for the youth.

Civilian Housing

In the high desert, devoid of trees, it was necessary to build sod houses of earth. The "soddie" was insulated for summer heat and warmth in the winter. In spite of a few snakes and spiders, the sod house was quite popular at the time. Farmers who plowed the fields were called "sod-busters." The Homestead Act of 1860 gave qualified settlers 160 acres to farm. Acreages were fenced off, but cattlemen wanted open range. Range wars erupted.

Some poor people in Boise City were housed in tents or shanties, in hard times. Others were more fortunate and afforded log houses.

The O'Farrell cabin was the first house built in Boise in 1863. The cabin served as a house of worship and school. John A. O' Farrell erected the log cabin. A monument of the O'Farrell Cabin is set in stone near the edifice. The cabin still stands outside the gates of the old fort.

The Costin cabin was built east of Boise by Isaac Costin the same year Major Lugenbeel erected Fort Boise in Idaho Territory. Costin crafted the log cabin using full dove-tail joinery in the corners. He dwelled in the cabin for a time but later used it as an out-building.

The Mayor Logan Adobe House was built in 1865 for Thomas E. Logan. Adobe bricks, called "adobies," were made of mud and straw, which was sun-dried. Commonly used as Boise dwellings, adobe houses are non-existent in the Pacific Northwest today.

The Richard Adleman House is typical of the Boise homes built in the period 1870-1896. He migrated from Germany to New York City in 1854 with his parents. Adleman ran a saloon in Boise. He also worked as a miner and a volunteer fireman. He served in the Union Army during the Civil War.

The Fort and Boise City grew. There was a romance between the two. Fort Boise was built near the town of Boise City and the people were protected there from Indian uprisings. Fort Boise was a job source for the people living in Boise City. Houses were very primitive in the beginning.

Boise City was growing. Men outnumbered the women five to one. Fort Boise was the center of social activities in Boise City. The biggest dances, parties and social events were held there.

Lovers might have been seen riding horses on grounds along Cottonwood Creek. Mule deer, starved by the heavy snows, came to Fort

103

Building #1 was an officer's barracks on Officer's Row. The old barracks served as a doctor's residence for a time. Recently, the Veteran's Administration used this building for Human Resource Services, but is now the Regional Counsel & Employee Education Services building.   Courtesy Veterans Administration

Building #4 was built of hewn stone, quarried at Table Rock, east of Boise, by the Oregon Volunteers in 1870 at Fort Boise as an officers' quarter. It housed U.S. Cavalry Officers to defend the local citizenry from Indian uprising. Now deserted, a rumor on grounds is the old relic is haunted.   Courtesy Veterans Admin.

Building #6 was built in 1863 as the Quartermaster Building. It was built of hewn stone blocks, weighing 25-1,000 pounds each. Walls were insulated with rock rubble and adobe. It was the first insulated building in Idaho and is currently used as an Eye Clinic.
Courtesy of the Veteran's Administration

Grave-stones of unsung heroes Frank Whittle of the Washington Volunteers and Sam Sutherland, 1st Oregon Cavalry, killed by Indians while serving their country during the Indian Wars and are buried in the cemetery at the rear of the Fort Boise grounds, Boise, Idaho.   (Courtesy of the Veteran's Administration)

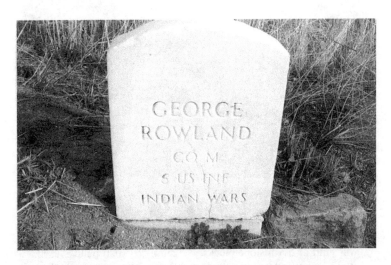

George Rowland of Company M 6th U.S. Cavalry is buried in the cemetery back of the Fort Boise grounds in Boise. U.S. Cavalry soldier George Rowland was killed while serving America during the Indian Wars. (Author photo)

The O'Farrell Cabin was the very first house built in Boise serving as a house of worship and school. John A. O' Farrell erected the cabin of logs. The cabin still stands outside the gates of the old fort. (Courtesy Veteran's Administration)

Boise in droves during the winter time. Since then, cougars, elk and moose have been seen in Boise's outskirts.

The first Idaho Territory capital was Lewiston. In 1864 Boise City became the territorial capital of Idaho Territory, taking in a 60,000 square miles expanse that is present day Idaho, Montana and Wyoming. Boise grew at a rapid rate with the population explosion in Idaho from thousands of miners rushed to the Boise Basin, during the "Idaho Gold Rush." Many settlers came into Boise, off the Oregon Trail. Boise was the largest city on the trail. In 1864 Boise had 1,685 residents. The population of Idaho City was 20,000 people at the time.

The Treaty of Boise in 1864 was written at the fort. The simple document said that the Shoshoni Indians gave up the Boise River drainage for care under the U.S. Government and were treated as a favored tribe however the treaty took away the Indians lifeblood. The treaty was never legally ratified. At a later date Governor Caleb Lyon wrote another treaty with the Bruneau Shoshoni.

Major Lugenbeel was appointed Assistant Provost Marshall of Oregon and Washington in Portland. Thompson took over his Command.

Indian Uprisings
In 1865, Indian troubles were breaking out in Oregon. Fort Boise used southern outposts to control the Indians: Camp Lyon, State militia camp was built near present day Jordan Valley, Oregon. Camp Three Forks Owyhee on Soldier Creek, near the South Fork of the Owyhee River outside of Jordan Valley was raised on the southwest base of South Mountain (originally Mt. Winthrop), in 1866, to house Indian prisoners.

Summer camps outside Fort Boise were established in the outer perimeter to contain these Indians. In the south were Camps Alvord, C.F.

Smith, Lander, and Reed in Oregon Territory. Camp Logan and Camp Watson lay to the north. General George Crook chased renegade Paiutes in the Owyhees. In 1866 J.H. Walker and the 14th Infantry killed 18 Indians in Bruneau country, taking 19 horses and antiquated weapons. In another skirmish in the Owyhees ten more Indians were killed.

Indian agent Hough moved 400 Bruneau River Shoshoni to Fort Hall Reservation for their own safety. They wanted provisions and blankets for the winter. Snake Indians that came in were also protected at Fort Boise. In 1867, 200 Indians in the Boise City vicinity waited in a camp for assignment. Later they were moved further north, so they could hunt and fish. 850 Bruneau Shoshonis and 150 Bannocks wintered at the camp above Boise City. Many died of measles or other diseases. In 1869 Governor Ballard ordered Indian Agent Powell to move the Shoshonis to Fort Hall and on March thirteenth Powell began the move.

In 1870 the United States Cavalry built a fort south of Blackfoot. Various denominations of American Churches sent missionaries to the Indians at Fort Hall. Catholic, Episcopal, Mormon and Presbyterian missionaries were assigned to the Indians. Episcopal missionaries built an boarding school for Indian children. A Catholic bishop initiated a cemetery for red and white men, alike. In 1891 Miss Frost started a Presbyterian mission school for the Paiute and Shoshoni children.

In 1876, Fort Boise was an outpost to dispatch the Militia to protect settlers during the Indian Wars. It was a post to house Brigadier General George Crook, who set up a base camp there, ready to route any Indian hostiles. Crook was an Indian fighter; his "long-knives" were successful in fighting the "horse warriors." He was respected by the red man, who called him "Grey Fox." He moved supplies using pack-trains. He utilized Indian scouts to track hostiles.

In 1877 Major Green and his U.S. Cavalry were dispatched from Fort Boise to fight the warring Nez Perce. Fort John Russell was a settler's fort from 1877-79 at Moscow, during the outbreak.

As the Nez Perce War ended, the Bannock War erupted in 1878. Captain Bernard and his troops, quartered at Fort Boise rode to Camas Prairie, in pursuit of the raging Indians. In 1879 Fort Boise was renamed, Boise Barracks. Idaho was admitted into the Union in 1890 and in 1912 the post closed.

In those days there was no cure for diseases like smallpox and a toll was taken upon immediate populations, especially the Indians, who had never been exposed to such European diseases. A tragic story is told of an anonymous army major, his wife and family who caught smallpox.

First the boy died. The Major went outside and yelled "smallpox," and disappeared back into the cabin. As they tended him, his mother died of the pox. Four more children died and the Major. To avoid the disease, the bodies were lassoed and dragged behind a horse to open graves. The Major being last, wrapped himself in his blanket laid down and died outside their cabin, to be drug away. The cabin was burned to avoid the spread of smallpox. This incident took place at Fort Boise.

Fort Boise Cemetery

The original cemetery behind Fort Boise was located near Cottonwood Creek from 1869-1903. Soldiers were buried there. A flash-flood in 1903 caused the creek to overflow its banks and wash out some of the graves. In 1910 the remaining graves were moved one fourth of a mile to a nearby hillside where the military cemetery is today. Grave stones

109

Sioux Indian chief delegation in Omaha is on route to Washington. (Front row, left to right) Sioux Indian chiefs pictured are Sitting Bull, Swift Bear, Spotted Tail and Red Cloud. (Back row) Agents Julius Meyer, William Garnett, and Louis Bordeaux are standing.

(Courtesy A.P.)

Old stone guard station entrance to Fort Boise stands where a guard was posted 24 /7. Anyone entering Fort Boise had to pass through this gate. All civilians, soldiers, or vendors papers were checked at this guard station before entering.

Courtesy Veterans Administration

110

The Mayor Logan Adobe House was built in 1865 for Thomas E. Logan. Adobe bricks or adobies were made of mud and straw, then sun-dried, commonly used as Boise dwellings. They are non-existent in the Northwest, today.   (Author photo)

The Richard Adleman House was built after 1870. Adleman came from Germany in 1854. He ran a saloon in Boise and worked as a miner and a volunteer fireman. Adleman fought in the Union Army during the Civil War.   (Author photo)

read Civil War, Indian Wars and Spanish American War. Many of the gravestones are from the original units that first arrived with Major Lugenbeel, July 4, 1863, to combat the Indians. In 1998, nearly a century later, a ditch was dug along the road near the original cemetery in order to put in a cement drainage ditch. Two partial skeletons and a coffin had been missed, were unearthed at that time and moved to the present cemetery.

The post closed in 1912, along with other smaller forts in America. It was reopened for other wars. The Veterans Hospital took over in 1930. The 33 acres, Fort Boise grounds today, includes the Lugenbeel U. S. Army Reserve Center. At least three old buildings from 1863 remain and the O'Farrell settler's cabin and stone guard-house.

Fort Boise artifacts which were found on the grounds are on display in the V.A. Medical Building. Old bullets, Minnie balls, a belt buckle, a straight razor, Civil War tokens, a chisel, a horse-shoe, an adobe brick, bottles and a sword sheath can be seen there. Idaho State Archeologist, Tom Green and other archeologists did excavations there.

The U.S. Federal Building, Internal Revenue Service and U.S. Court House are located on the old fort grounds. The V.A. Hospital, dozens of outbuildings, a pharmacy, dental clinic and police are on grounds, The Elks Rehab Hospital and Idaho State Veterans Home are also located there. The Fort Boise Park Community center has 6 lighted tennis courts, 3 lighted softball fields, and a regulation baseball diamond. Fort Boise Middle School, Mountain Cove School, a Skateboard Park and Boise Little Theater are on the grounds. The final scene of "Bronco Billy," Clint Eastwood's wild-west movie was filmed there in October, 1979. A major thoroughfare in north Boise is Fort Street, named after the old fort, by the city. Fort Boise is on the National Register of Historic Places as a Historic District.

War Memorial ol Colonel Pinkney Lugenbeel, Founder of Fort
Boise. Col. Lugenbeel died in Detroit, Michigan March 18, 1886.
Photo Courtesy of Idaho State Historical Society.

In the high desert, devoid of trees, it was necessary to build sod houses of earth. The "soddie" was insulated for summer heat and warmth in the winter. Farmers that plowed the fields were called "sod-busters."   (Courtesy of Ned Eddins)

The Costin cabin was built east of Boise in 1863 by Isaac Costin. He crafted the log cabin using full dove-tail joinery in the corners and dwelled in the cabin for a time. He later used the cabin as an out-building.   (Author photo)

Chapter Eight

Indian Wars

A pony soldier was issued a horse, saddle, bridle, dark blue tunics, light blue trousers, belt, socks, boots, neckerchief, cap and jacket. Weapons issued were a 45 caliber rifle, 45 caliber pistol, ammunition and saber.

The life of a soldier was hard back then. Spending hours in the saddle, lacking sleep, they were exposed to the hot sun, wind, and rain. Winters were equally as grueling, out in the elements, enduring blizzards, ice, mud, and wind in the line of duty.

The bluecoats had duties besides combat. The Army wrote treaties with the Indians. They smoked the peace pipe with them and gave peaceable Indian chiefs peace medals from the U.S. President that bore his image.

President George Washington originated the peace medal and gave these medals to peaceable Indian chiefs. This practice was carried out by twenty U.S. Presidents in succession. Some of the treaties held, but others were broken.

Fighting broke out between Indians and the whites. The U.S. Cavalry was called in to intervene. Battles ensued in Idaho and surrounding territories. The Cayuse Indians warred from 1848-1850.

Two Washington miners were killed by renegade Indians in 1858. Palouse Indians stole emigrants' cattle, touting them to react. Coeur d'Alene, Palouse and Spokane Indians came to the brink of war. Major Steptoe led a Military Campaign against them.

Chief Winnemucca II of the Nevada Northern Paiutes was born around 1820. His was commonly known as Poito. He was less trusting of the white man than his father, Chief Truckee. Indian Agents had shorted the Paiute people of rations at Fort McDermott and Pyramid Lake for some time. The people were starving. So when it came to the Paiute War of 1860, Chief Winnemucca was a proponent.

The Paiute War was between Northern Paiutes, some Bannock and Shoshoni and white settlers that took place in 1860 near Pyramid Lake (now Nevada).

The war began with violent attacks on settlers ending in two battles where nearly 80 whites were killed. The number of Paiutes that died in the fights was unrecorded. Smaller raids followed and finally, a peace was reached in August of 1860, without a treaty.

Gold was discovered in 1862 in the Boise Basin. Miners infringed on Indian land, having found gold on the Nez Perce Reservation and in the Black Hills.

The gold-rush to Idaho City, Silver City, along the Salmon River and Coeur d'Alene River opened up mining, encouraging migration of thousands of miners into Idaho Territory. The tent city of Lewiston was named capital. Idaho City had become a boom town with a population larger than any in the northwest.

Prospectors led by George Grimes left Auburn, in Oregon Territory, mid-July of 1862. They employed some Snake Indians as guides to the Boise Basin. Six miles outside Bannock (present day Idaho City) near Centerville, they discovered gold. They were ambushed by Bannock Indians and Grimes was murdered.

Sioux Chief Sitting Bull was a Hunkpapa Medicine Man of the Teton Sioux. The Medicine-Man had a dream. In his vision Sitting Bull saw soldiers descending on them like grasshoppers. The soldiers fell down on the ground in defeat.   (Courtesy A.P.)

Lt. Colonel George Custer was transferred out West to head the Seventh Cavalry. He led the attack on the Indians at the Battle of Washita. Custer was hated by the Indians. Elizabeth "Libbie" Bacon Custer was married to the Lt. Colonel. She enjoyed dining with her husband in the field.   (Courtesy A. P.)

Original photo of Thomas Ward Custer, the brother of George Custer, fought in his ranks. Tom died with his brother during the siege at the Little Bighorn. 210 soldiers died in that battle.

(Courtesy Theron Ludlow)

118

Sitting Bull was attacked by Custer and Reno's forces. It was Sitting Bull's warriors that defeated George Armstrong Custer at the Little Bighorn. Courtesy of Azusa Publishing Co, L.L.C.

That incident along with the Ward Massacre created a dire need for a military fort in the vicinity. The gold strike had caused many hundreds more miners to flock to the area.

In 1867 the Comanche went on the warpath. The long battle that ensued was called the Blackhawk Wars. Chief Quanah and 400 Comanche were last to relent and entered Fort Sill, driving 1500 head of horses onto the reservation.

Shoshoni Indians were forced to move onto reservations by 1870. Mountain Sheep-eater Shoshoni Chief Eagle-Eye refused. General Howard pursued Eagle-Eye during the Snake War in 1866. The Army quit looking for him after a false report of his death. Chief Eagle-Eye chose to remain on the land around Dry Buck and Timber Butte, an old obsidian source of the Shoshoni, near present day Emmet, Idaho. He and his people engaged in the mining and timber business and were friendly to the white man. He remained there until 1904, before going to the Fort Hall Reservation.

Sioux Indians were Algonquin speakers of Northern Canada that expanded into Montana and the Dakotas. They were a warring tribe and fought over territory. The Sioux were enemies of the Shoshoni, also the Blackfoot, Crow and Ute.

A young Sioux Indian experienced his vision quest. In a revelation, he saw a horse, whose hooves did not touch the ground. The horse floated as it galloped and changed colors as did the attire of his rider. The Indian rode effortlessly, seeing grass, sky and trees. He was "Crazy Horse," named for his father.

Crazy Horse had a dream of an incident between Sioux and white man that troubled him. (1854) a Minnenjou Sioux, named "High

Forehead," shot a Mormon's cow near the Fort Laramie trading post. Army Lieutenant John Grattan decided to teach the Sioux a lesson. He took 34 soldiers with two cannons to annihilate the Sioux. They never returned. Later, all 35 men were found massacred.

Colonel Chivington and the Colorado Volunteers ambushed Chief Black Kettle's Cheyenne tribe at the Sand Creek Massacre in 1864. Chief Black Kettle's life was spared.

In 1865, 1866 and 1868, the U.S. Government wrote treaties with the Sioux Nation. In the treaty of 1868 the Great Sioux Reservation was born. Later,

In 1875 the Red Cloud Delegation visited President Grant in Washington D.C. Chiefs Red Cloud, Sitting Bull, Spotted Tail, and Swift Bear of the Sioux Nation attended. They met with the President of the United States about the purchase of the Black Hills.

In 1876 the Sioux Indians were ordered to the Rosebud Reservation or were considered hostiles. General Crook embarked from Fort Walla-Walla to engage the Cheyenne and Sioux Indians. Shoshoni Indians fell in behind Crook's column to give battle to their old enemy the Sioux. Crook attacked the Cheyenne and Sioux encampment on Rosebud Creek but met defeat.

Sioux Chief Red Cloud gained respect as a warrior. He waged Red Cloud's War against the soldier forts and miners along the Bozeman Trail, which cut through Sioux hunting grounds. He came in to Fort Laramie and signed the 1868 Peace Treaty, relinquishing the Black Hills Red Cloud was with the Sioux delegation to Washington D.C. in 1875. He was an important chief orator and statesman for the Sioux Nation.

121

Photograph of Custer's officers and friends taken at a family gathering, when Custer was in charge of Fort Abraham Lincoln. George Custer is shown with long locks. The Indians gave him the nick-name of "Long Hair."   (Courtesy A.P.)

Original photo of Major Fredrick W. Benteen, who came to the aid of Major Reno, when he was in trouble on the Little Big-horn. He hated his superior officer, George Custer. Benteen was one soldiers that made it out alive.   (Courtesy Theron Ludlow)

Sioux War Chief Gall was the
Sioux chief that led the raid of
hundreds of warriors on George
Armstrong Custer and routed Reno
at the Battle of the Little Bighorn.
Gall was Sitting Bull's adopted brother.
Photo Courtesy of Azusa Publishing,
L.L.C.

War Chief Red Cloud
closed the Bozeman Trail
defeating the U.S. Army
Photo Courtesy of Azusa
Publishing, L.L.C.L.L.C.

Sitting Bull in the Sioux language was Tantanka Iyotanka. He had a dream. In his vision he saw soldiers descending onto them like grasshoppers, but the Soldiers fell on the ground in defeat.

Lt. Colonel George Armstrong Custer was a famous figure in the old west and fought as a general for the Union in the Civil War. He was a Civil War General for the North at an early age, nicknamed the "Boy General." He married Elizabeth "Libbie" Bacon. Custer was stationed out West to lead the 7th Cavalry.

Libbie dined with George in the field, while his brother Tom and nephew, Boston rode in his ranks. Custer led the attack on the Indians at the Battle of Washita, where he killed Chief Black Kettle. He was loathed by the Indians and for some reason was hated by Captain Fredrick Benteen, one of his officers.

Custer's cavalry had ridden all night in order to reach Rosebud Sioux Indian Village in South Dakota. The over confident Custer would not take the advice of his Indian scouts and retreat because of the Indian's large numbers... His Arikara and Crow Indian scouts prepared to die, knowing their fate. He apparently could not believe that they were heading for disaster. Instead he was eager to massacre these Indians. Custer was psyched up talking to his scouts, bolstering his troops, riding among them. The general was very excited about fighting the battle.

There is narrative about Custer's Crow scouts. As the story goes, the Crow scouts at the Little Bighorn changed out of their army uniforms into their Indian garb. When questioned by Custer, they explained that they wanted to die in their own garb. The general got very angry and dismissed them.

On June 25, 1876, George Armstrong Custer led five companies of his Seventh Cavalry in hot pursuit of the Sioux Indians along the Little Bighorn River. Custer made a fatal mistake dividing his companies into three groups. At the Little Bighorn Custer led two companies. Major Marcus A. Reno took two companies and Captain Fredrick Benteen headed up one company of men to southwest Glen Creek, then rode along the east side of the river. Captain Benteen was to stay close and if no Indians could be found, return to ranks.

The Cheyenne Indians remembered "Long Hair" from his massacre of Chief Black Kettle's village. They hated Custer with a passion.

Sitting Bull had gathered the largest army of Indians ever assembled on the Columbia Plateau. 2,000 Arapaho, Blackfoot, Cheyenne and Sioux Indian warriors under Chiefs Sitting Bull, Crazy Horse, Gall, Red Cloud, and Spotted Tail were ready for any attack.

The temperature was fast approaching triple digits as Custer's three companies rode hard charging Chief Sitting Bull's village. Custer and Reno's offensive approached both ends of the Rosebud Sioux village. Sitting Bull's adopted brother, Chief Gall and sub-chief under him, led the attack. Major Marcus Reno attacked at the other end of the encampment. Chief Gall routed Major Reno and met Custer's forces head on with hundreds of Sioux warriors for a decisive frontal attack.

As General Custer's battalion fought for their lives, Major Reno and Captain Benteen were engaged in battle. Reno was in trouble. Captain Benteen rallied and came to his defense. Reno's army, reinforced by Benteen's men had losses but survived to live and fight another day.

Original photo of U.S. Army officer, George Carey rode under Lieutenant Colonel Custer Armstrong at the Battle of the Little Bighorn against the Sioux Indians.
(Courtesy Theron Ludlow)

Mountain Crow Scout, Hairy Moccasin enlisted in the U.S. Army, 7th Infantry under Lt. James Bradley on April 10, 1876. He scouted for Gibbons, Miles and Custer. At the Little Bighorn he advised Custer of the large number of Sioux.(Courtesy A.P.)

Custer and his complement were outnumbered, surrounded by the Sioux Nation's cavalry. Two hundred ten men were massacred by the Sioux Indians at "Custer's Last Stand," in the Battle of the Little Bighorn. Sioux War-chiefs Gall and Crazy Horse were credited with conquering the 7th Cavalry. Custer died on June 25, 1876. A statue of George Armstrong Custer, mounted on his horse was erected near his old hometown in Monroe, Michigan.

Hairy Moccasin was a Mountain Crow Scout who volunteered under Lt. James Bradley's detachment of Indian Scouts. He served as scout for service for the U.S. Army 7th Cavalry under General Gibbons, General Howard, Captain Miles and Lt. Col. Custer. Hairy Moccasin was reported to have given the size and position of the Sioux encampment at the valley of the Little Bighorn.

Chief American Horse of the Ogallala Sioux was a warrior orator and diplomat to the government for his people. After the tragic Wounded Knee Uprising he became the leader of the Sioux delegation representing his people to Washington. American Horse was one of the Sioux Chiefs who later performed in Buffalo Bill's Wild West Show.

May 1877, Sitting Bull escaped to Canada. Around the same time Crazy horse surrendered at Fort Robinson. That year General Miles defeated a small band of Minnenjou Sioux, ending the war with the Sioux.

Native American Crow Indian, Hairy Moccasin and other Crow scouts honor Custer and those that fell with him. These Crow scouts pay Custer homage after his death at the Little Bighorn.

(Courtesy A. P.)

President Grover Cleveland peace medal (1885) was given to peaceable Indian chiefs. This one is silver in a beaded necklace from the author's personal collection. (Reverse side) It portrays an Indian and a white settler and PEACE.

(Author photo)

War-Chief Quanah Parker was the son of Chief Pete Nocona and white captive Cynthia Ann Parker. He rose to the rank of chief in the 1860 Comanche Wars. He led the attack of 900 warriors on Adobe Walls. (Courtesy A. P.)

Daughters of Comanche Chief Quanah Parker (Photo Courtesy of A.P.)

The Nez Perce

In 1800 the Nez Perce Country covered about seventeen million acres that became Idaho, Oregon and Washington. The area reached from the Bitterroot Mountains to the Blue Mountain Range. In 1805, the Nez Perce made up the largest tribe in the Columbia River Plateau, with a population of about 6,000 Native Americans in 300 camps and villages. Evidence of their habitation is the heavy rock writing in Hell's Canyon. Hundreds of scenic ancient petro-glyphs appear along the Snake River, on Hell's Canyon rock and walls.

The area teemed with bighorn sheep, bear, cougar, deer and elk which provided good hunting. The Nez Perce Indians were in place for thousands of years. These Indians fished in the Snake River region of Hell's Canyon and dwelled in the now present day northern Idaho, Oregon and Washington. Salmon runs provided a wealth of fish to fill the belly and to store in bundled cakes for winter. They were contacted by the Spanish explorers, and later, Lewis and Clark. Reverend Henry Spalding built his Presbyterian Mission School at Lapwai on Nez Perce ground. Trade had been established West with the Columbia River and Coastal Indians communicating by trade sign language.

An ancient fishing village has been found there by archeologists recently. The Wallowa Nez Perce today gather yearly for a Friendship Feast and Powwow, as did their ancestors in ancient days.

In 1840, a defender of the people was born to the Nez Perce. His name was In-mut-too-yah-lat-lat in the Chutepula (Nez Perce) tongue, meaning Thunder-Traveling-over-the-Mountains. His common name was Young Joseph. His father was called Old Chief Joseph. He was of the Wallam-wat-kin band of the Chutepula tribe. As a youth, young Joseph attended the Spalding Mission School, run by Rev. Henry Spalding. He spent several years there, before returning to Wallowa in Oregon territory in 1847. His father was quite ill then and Joseph took on duties as peacetime village chief and leader.

Old Joseph (Tuekakas) wouldn't have anything to do with the soldier peace council. He warned Young Joseph not to accept gifts from the white man for they might Claim the gifts were trade for their land. He also told his son not to give up the land of their fathers. He did not trust anyone who would buy and sell land. The Indians believed that they could not possess the land, but just manage it. But in 1855 the Steven's treaty was signed by the Cayuse, Nez Perce, Umatilla and the Walla-Walla. Lawyer signed, as did Looking Glass and reluctantly, by Tuekakas. This treaty allowed the Nez Perce to keep most of Wallowa but the government would soon break their treaty.

Chief Looking Glass earned his named because of the signal mirror he wore on a leather thong around his neck. He was a sub-chief under Young Joseph.

10,000 miners and settlers disregarded the treaty and trespassed on lands of the Nez Perce. Indian agents in 1868 demanded the Nez Perce leave their scenic Walla-Walla Valley that teemed with creeks, rivers and game with the beautiful Wallowa Mountains in the background, for a Lapwai Reservation. Young Joseph and his father fought this idea but Lawyer signed the treaty. By 1870 Washington pushed to place all Indians on reservations. Some went peaceably, many rebelled.

Young Chief Joseph was a handsome, stately Nez Perce Indian. He became an orator and a statesman. Joseph was polygamous, however. He would take four wives and fathered nine children. When Old Joseph died in 1871, Young Joseph expressed his feelings in this poem of his father.

131

I buried him in the valley

of the winding waters. (Wallowa)

I love that land more

than all the rest of the world.

After his father's death, Young Joseph became chief of the Wallowa Nez Perce. He came to be a great orator, statesman and warchief. Chief Joseph was known as a noble red man to both Indian and white man.

The council meeting at Lapwai began on May 2, 1877. Joseph (the orator), narrated the wrongs to his people and the need for them to be treated fairly. Joseph stated that he did not speak with a forked tongue. General Howard urged them to go on the reservation. The government had taken Joseph's lands, horses and cattle, giving him many reasons to rebel. General Howard broke his promise to Chief Joseph, ordering the Nez Perce, with livestock, onto the reservation in 30 days, then reordered the soldiers to round up the Indians. General Howard had promised him that they could keep Wallowa Valley, (Winding water in the Nez Perce language) but the army took over their land.

The Nez Perce had been friendly and also fair to the explorers, the fur trappers and to the white settlers. Now, the pendulum was swinging the other way. Too many white men were coming. The white man and his armies were pushing them off their lands. Chiefs Joseph, White Bird and Too-hul-hut-sote held a grand council at Lake Tolo at the head of Rocky Canyon. Some wanted war. The statesman, Joseph pleaded for peace but was accused of cowardice. Some expected military intervention. In Rocky Canyon they held festivities with dancing, stick games, horse Races and parades. They took advantage of their freedom at the time.

Unruly young Nez Perce braves drank "firewater" that they had gotten from settlers. Braves had prepared for war, by purchasing guns and ammunition from the whites, earlier. Walaitits, a brave whose father had been killed by the white man cried for revenge. Someone urged Wailtits to go and kill the white men who had murdered his father. Wailtits, Red Moccasin, and Swan Necklace drank until they were intoxicated. The three braves became belligerent and readied for war. These were all members of Chief White Bird's band. Joseph and Ollokut were gone during this incident.

The braves rode to the Salmon River and Slate Creek on June 13, 1877 and lay in wait behind rocks where they shot Richard Devine in his open doorway. Next, they rode to John Day shooting Henry Elfers, Robert Bland and Harry Beckroge dead. The Nez Perce War had begun. When they returned, White Bird jumped onto his horse and rode through the camp, urging war and his braves carried out more raids.

Toohulhutsote, who had been jailed by the army, joined the insurgents and went out to kill and plunder with the others. This action had sparked the initial phase of the Nez Perce War. Many of the tribe returned to Lapwai Reservation. Joseph wanted peace and to return to the reservation. Ollokut remained silent. Three Eagles said that he could not go back and would fight. It was too late. The damage had been done.

The settlers hearing rumors of the Indian war began making preparations. The settlers at Slate Creek were undermanned with few firearms. There were 40 women and children and 23 men. They hurriedly built a stockade and decided that someone should go for help.

Tolo (Alanewa), wife of Tawe (Red Wolf), a peaceable Indian woman, was elected. Tolo traveled the 25 miles to Florence, a mining town, and cried for help. She returned with twelve armed miners to Slate Creek. A monument, near Grangeville was erected in her honor.

The tribe had to eat so Joseph and his chiefs moved into White Bird Canyon where they rounded up their cattle for butchering. White Bird Canyon is very grassy with steep rolling hills. The terrain is uneven with buttes, knolls and ridges. The creek ran through the bottom land.

General Howard had sent to Fort Vancouver and Fort Walla Walla for more cavalry and infantry units which were moved by steamship up river to Nez Perce Country. At Fort Lapwai troops received rigid training in Indian fighting. On June 15, two companies under Captain Perry arrived at Fort Lapwai from Fort Vancouver.

On June 16, Perry and companies F & H, a complement of ninety eight men, departed Fort Lapwai for White Bird Canyon. The soldiers had lost much sleep, being in the saddle for days. It was drizzling rain, as the rode first to Cottonwood and on to Grangeville.

Joseph's scouts observed the procession and it was no surprise to them that the soldiers were coming to fight. The U. S. Cavalry led by Captain Perry and his militia and scouts arrived in White Bird Canyon at about midnight the evening of June 16.

At dawn the next morning June 17, 1877, Perry and his two companies, eleven volunteers and scouts rode down the steep hill into the canyon, a 3,000 foot descent to creek level. About 300 yards out, troops led by Lieutenant Theller saw six Nez Perce Indians on horseback moving toward them, carrying the white flag of truce.

A rifle cracked then another broke the silence, as Ad Chapman, Theller's scout fired two rounds that struck the dirt near the flag bearers.

Horse-mounted Indian observers scattered on the field returning fire. It was a standoff. Perry's men and volunteers fired on the Indians and began the clash.

Nez Perce warriors stripped down to loin-cloths and moccasins, for war, according to their tradition. Joseph, on the other hand, remained in war-shirt, leggings, and moccasins for battle. Joseph had no choice, but to fight. An old Indian war slogan was, "it is a good day to die." The Indians fought, seemingly with no fear, taking cover behind rocks and knolls, as did the militia.

Lieutenant Theller attacked, followed by the volunteers. Joseph ordered the horse herd to be taken down to the river, behind the bluff. The women and children broke camp. He divided his force into two groups under Chiefs Ollokut and Two Moons. They led the charge, attacking from two sides. Joseph blocked attack across the center. The army had cannons, Gatling guns, howitzers, rifles, pistols and bayonets at their disposal during this campaign. The Indians had only 50 guns, bows and arrows, possibly lances, tomahawks and steel or stone knives. Chiefs Too-hul-hut-sote and White Bird fought bravely.

The old Indian trick of running horses through the enemy's ranks divided the soldiers. Soon, they were in disarray and, confused. Horses ran free. Smoke and gunfire filled the air. Rifle cracks came nonstop... The Indians uttered shrill Indian war-cries. The horses were spooked, so the soldiers had to dismount causing Perry and his men began to retreat.

Chief White Bird pursued Perry and his men as they retreated to Cottonwood. Firing on them, White Bird followed them all the way to Johnson's ranch before turning back, to take spoils on the field. The Battle of White Bird Creek left 33 soldiers dead and 7 wounded.

General Howard, with 400 troops and 100 scouts, had left camp at Lake Tolo for Fort Lapwai. On the 23rd he sent Trimble and his men to Slate Creek to defend the citizens. The general awaited word of the whereabouts of the hostiles and for reinforcements from Lewiston. Howard pushed his men from there to overtake the Indians.

On June 25th Howard split his column and advanced to Johnson's ranch. Upon reaching Grangeville was joined by Perry and his remaining troops, Howard advanced to White Bird Canyon.

Joseph had fewer loses. Joseph's Nez Perce had the victory, delivering the second most severe defeat to the army since the Little Big Horn. At this juncture, people feared that Joseph would conquer Howard and unite with the Columbia Plateau Indians and become unbeatable. The Nez Perce War was underway.

Joseph returned to his lodge to learn that he had become a father, a daughter had been born. Chief Looking Glass arrived with more warriors. Joseph had begun an exodus that would continue for days, weeks and months. Chief Looking Glass was camped on Cottonwood Creek. He pulled up stakes and moved to the Clearwater, trying to avoid war. That night the Indians held a victory dance. The following day, in a brilliant tactical maneuver, Joseph exited White Bird Canyon in a wide circle, making tracking them very difficult. Using this method, Joseph avoided contact with Major Green's three companies of cavalry and twenty Bannock scouts, coming from Fort Boise. The army did not engage Joseph and his warriors again until Cottonwood was reached. The chiefs had nearly 300 warriors to lead into battle. June 22nd

General Howard, with 400 troops and 100 scouts, had left camp at Lake Tolo for Fort Lapwai. On the 23rd he sent Trimble and his men to Slate Creek to defend the citizens. The general awaited word of the

136

whereabouts of the hostiles and for reinforcements from Lewiston. Howard pushed his men to overtake the Indians. On June 25th Howard split his column and advanced to Johnson's ranch. He was joined by Captain Perry in Grangeville. Howard advanced to White Bird Canyon.

On June 26th, at White Bird Canyon, the rain had washed the dirt from the shallow graves, exposing the dead soldier's bodies. Howard had them reburied. The corpses had been stripped of clothing, but Joseph's warriors had taken no scalps. As Howard reburied the dead, Captain Paige climbed to the crest of a high ridge. From that viewpoint he surveyed the Indians, beyond the Salmon, retreating. Miles arrived at White Bird. On July 9 Howard followed Joseph's path of retreat.

Joseph had made camp at Horseshoe Bend and prepared to cross the Salmon River. Ollokut and White Bird also wanted to cross the Salmon and flee to out distance the general. These chiefs had the mind-set that if they could escape Howard's jurisdiction, they would be free of war. The tribe was joined at Horseshoe Bend by Five Wounds, Rainbow, and other Nez Perce warriors who were back from the buffalo hunt. The chief council planned their defense. General Howard, 700 Cavalry and Bannock scout, Buffalo Horn pursued the Nez Perce on June 28. Joseph crossed the Salmon River baiting the General, to cut off his supply lines.

Five Wounds and Rainbow remained behind as snipers slowed Howard down on the afternoon of June 28th. The snipers took pot-shots at the soldiers as they approached the crossing; the soldiers returned fire with their long range rifles. The Indians disappeared. Joseph's people crossed with little trouble, but Howard had a tough time with the big guns and supply wagons. Joseph re-crossed the river at Craig's Ferry and attacked Howard from the rear causing many losses. Joseph made a temporary treaty with the soldiers, trading stock and supplies with them.

Howard and the remaining soldiers were on the move; many of Joseph's tribe went back to the reservation. Others joined Looking Glass, who was camped on the Clearwater just 4 miles south of Kooskia. Many braves had left there to join the hostiles. Getting wind of this, General Howard ordered a surprise raid on the camp of Chief Looking Glass.

Captain Whipple and his complement rode to the camp hoping to capture them and take them to Mount Idaho. The soldiers reached camp at dawn. Chief Looking Glass came to meet them displaying a white flag. Whipple asked the chief to surrender. White Bird refused and one of the Captain's men began firing on the camp.

The Indians returned fire and Looking Glass joined them as they retreated, shooting back. Looking Glass joined Joseph and addressed the chiefs, vowing to fight the Bluecoats. Looking Glass had sent word to the Indian agent that he and 40 warriors wanted to come in to the Lapwai Reservation. Howard's order and the attack by Whipple and his men caused the chief to revert from being peaceable to a warring Indian. Looking Glass's band proceeded to join Joseph on the Clearwater River. Meanwhile, some of his braves told some Chinese workers that they were declaring war on the white man and would commence to raid on the Clearwater in 48 hours. Because of the threat, Mount Idaho sent out 20 volunteers to the Clearwater.

The army in the meantime was close behind Joseph's braves. He traveled from Craig's Mountain to Cottonwood. Joseph camped two miles north of Cottonwood. He positioned warriors on both sides of the road.

Captain McConville was riding hard from Slate Creek, to reinforce Whipple's command. On July 4th Indians ran from his soldiers at Norton, acting fearful, however, McConville had been ordered to take a different route. Had he followed the decoys, they would have been ambushed.

Captain Whipple had sent Lieutenant Rains and his detachment to scout for Joseph's Nez Perce on the same day. He was to report back if they found anything. Instead, Rains and his men rode right into Joseph's trap. Caught in the crossfire, the soldiers dismounted and ran for cover. The ambushed soldiers dropped one by one from the warrior's bullets, until all were dead. Joseph lost 9 braves in the skirmish at Cottonwood.

When Whipple arrived and knew from a distance that he was too late to save them. He placed his men in combat position not far from the massacre site. On the same July 4, the hostiles attacked Whipple and his troops in Norton, at Cottonwood House.

Perry and his troops waited hours for another attack. Instead, Joseph's warriors had attacked Mount Idaho. On July 5th the Indians sent up smoke signals, in three billowy puffs, from a plateau about three miles away. Randall and Evans attempted to break through the hostiles lines. Both were killed. McConville arrived too late to save Randall. July 6th, to prevent a massacre, Simpson and Whipple rode with their complement to the citizens' rescue. July 9th some warriors again attacked Mount Idaho and fought Major George Shearer's men. Howard had done a reversal, turning his troops about. He ordered a night march to join Perry reaching Grangeville by July 9.

During the retreat, Chief Joseph had led his whole village, beginning with an estimated 750 tribes-people. There were 400 warriors mounted on a massive herd of splendid Appaloosa horses into battle. The Nez Perce had bred and raised the beautiful Appaloosa. Their herd count reached 2,000 head along with other breeds, and pack mules. Horse-drawn travois pulled lodge-poles, carrying goods, hides and infants. As their horses were lost or stolen in battle, the Nez Perce rounded them up and stole more to replenish their stock.

Thinking they were far ahead of Howard's army, Joseph made camp and rested near Cottonwood Creek at the Clearwater River, where, he joined Looking Glass. Their horses grazed on the grassy hillsides. They fished and hunted to fill their bellies, while young braves raided small farms stealing cattle and horses. The Indians held a pow-wow and war dance. They played stick games and raced their horses. By accident a few volunteers discovered the unsuspecting Indians in their leisure. This was on July 11th across the Clearwater River. They surveyed the Indians holding horse races, as part of their festivities. The Battle of the Clearwater ensued. Toohulhutsote led 24 warriors across the river to meet Howard's attack. Other braves rushed to join Tuhulhutsote.

Howard had 400 men and 182 scouts. The soldiers dug in and built rock barriers. Howard ordered the attack, led by Perry and Whipple on their right and left flanks. The hostiles were caught in the middle. The Indians caught one line of soldiers in their crossfire. 400 soldiers rushed to their aid. The Indians met the charge. Joseph rode along his lines, giving war-cries and encouraging his warriors to fight. White Bird did the same. Their voices could be heard above the din. One warrior appeared on a ridge in rifle range, dancing and waving a red blanket, touting the soldiers. During the melee the Indians chanted eerie death and scalp chants. Rifle fire and howitzer bursts showered the Nez Perce. Indians continued their shouts and war-cries through the night.

At dawn, when the pack-trains arrived the Nez Perce were quick to attack, killing two. Indians made sallies on foot and horseback. The fighting was heavy. A cloud of acrid gun-smoke shrouded the field. War-cries and rebel yells filled the air. During the fighting a calamity

140

occurred, when Company B and the 21st Infantry behind the two mistook each other for the enemy. They began firing on each other. Finally Lieutenant Leary of the 4th Artillery ran out between the two lines with his rifle held by two hands in the air, shouting cease fire. Miller and Perry made an assault on the spring held by Indian snipers, July 12th. The men's canteens had gone dry and they were parched. The army gained control of the spring. There was a heavy barrage of fire that afternoon but the soldiers pushed the Indians back. The fighting had hasted over 30 hours and the warriors succeeded in defending their camp.

Captain Miles arrived with 200 more men. Joseph had been overseeing the women, packing up the goods and teepees. With Miles arrival Howard had 600 soldiers to face 100 Nez Perce warriors. Howard launched a full frontal charge. Their backs to the deep and swift Clearwater River, the Indians fled in retreat, leaving food cooking and lodges standing. In all Howard had 13 dead and 23 wounded, while Joseph claimed 4 dead and 6 wounded. The Nez Perce were outnumbered six to one. Howard had the upper hand. In addition, he had Gatling Guns and Howitzers versus Joseph's warriors Winchesters.

On July 13 Howard's cavalry appeared on the bluffs overlooking Kamiah Valley. They rode down to the water's edge, where the last of the hostiles had completed crossing the deep and swift Clearwater River. Joseph's snipers fired on the soldiers across the river. Militia returned fire with Gatling guns and rifles. The snipers scattered the cavalry with their bullets, giving Joseph enough time to escape.

Joseph broke camp, four miles from Kamiah, and sent a messenger to Howard asking for terms of surrender. He said that he didn't want to leave the land of his father's or to bring misery on his people. The chiefs then sent No Heart, a Nez Perce warrior under a white flag, to speak with

Naw Min-Old Nez Perce warrior is adorned in his white trade beads and garb. Long before the white man coastal Indians devised a monetary system called wampum. Wampum was exchanged in trade, similar to a monetary system called bead money. (Courtesy I.H.S.L.)

General Howard about terms of surrender. Howard returned to Kamiah after hearing the news, but nothing became of it. The messenger and his wife surrendered.

The Nez Perce began their ascent up the Lolo Trail over the Bitterroot Mountains. The trek over the trail has been referred to as the Nez Perce' "Trail of Tears" for the hardships and struggles that they faced.

On July 16, Joseph met his tribesman, Red Heart as he was returning home from the "buffalo hunt" on the upper Missouri. He did not join Joseph, but continued on to Lapwai. Howard captured the group and claimed he had taken them prisoner at the Battle of the Clearwater. They stripped the peaceful band of personal belongings, guns and horses. They were marched to Lapwai and Fort Vancouver; where they were held until spring.

Joseph held a council on the Weippe Prairie, at the start of the Lolo Trail. Chiefs Looking Glass, Too-hul-hut-sote, and White Bird wanted to join the Crow Indians in "buffalo country." Looking Glass was convinced that they should escape to the land of the Crows. He was a dreamer. The Crow Indians had long been the enemies of the Nez Perce, yet he thought them to be their allies.

Joseph refused, not wanting to leave "the land of their fathers." It was Old Joseph's wish. The older chiefs opposed Joseph and threatened his life and accused him of being a coward. Actually Joseph was very brave and far from cowardice. Joseph was overruled, yet established as the true leader to lead the people to Canada. He made Pile of Clouds his war-leader. It was decided that messengers would be sent to chiefs Charlotte and Michel of the Flatheads and the Pend d' Orielle to attain permission to pass through their country in peace.

143

Unidentified Nez Perce Warriors (about the same time as the Nez Perce War) these braves wear the same garb and the same similar beads to Joseph. They are surely from the same time period but there doesn't seem to be much information on them.

(Courtesy I.H.S.L.)

White Bird Battle Ground Memorial is a shrine in memory of the soldiers and Indians that died here that fateful day. 34 soldiers died here with two wounded; the Nez Perce' had much fewer casualties. (Author photo)

White Bird Battleground is a famous landmark. Here on June 17, 1877 Nez Perce War Chief Joseph engaged the U.S. Army Cavalry in combat. The U.S. Cavalry was defeated on this hill by the Nez Perce. (Author Photo)

145

About 3 miles from what is now Orofino, in Idaho Territory, forty or fifty warriors held back as a rear guard. A trap had been set by the Nez Perce. Trees had been sawed as obstacles to drop cross their path of retreat. Major Mason almost fell for the ambush, but a rifle shot from McConville's troops warned them of trouble in the area. One of his scouts was found dead, two injured and two more were taken captive.

As the Nez Perce traveled down Lolo Canyon, their progress was impeded by an obstruction. A bulwark, named Fort Fizzle, blocked their path, July 25th. The structure had been built by Captain Charles C. Rawn with the help of 44 soldiers. It blocked the trail access to the Bitterroot Valley. He recruited about 100 settlers and 30 additional soldiers to guard against Indians. The structure was three feet high and a rifle trench was dug. Rawn held a council with Joseph, White Bird and Looking Glass. The chiefs had friends in Montana and had traded at Missoula. They said they would pass and no one would be hurt. Rawn would accept their proposal only if they surrendered and turned over their arms, ammunition and horses.

The chiefs refused the offer. Captain Rawn wanted another council on the morrow. He would not otherwise grant safe passage. Looking Glass and a few braves met with him the next day, with no answer resulting. Looking Glass said he would have an answer the next morning but Joseph knew that Chief Charlotte of the Flatheads would not come to their aid. The farmers left for their homes. The Nez Perce did not want to fight them. The next day Captain Rawn heard the Indians singing, high on a ridge along the side of the cliff, as they moved in single file over the mountain. They had fooled Rawn. The Indians mused as they rode along toward the Bitterroots.

In the Bitterroots, the Nez Perce bought coffee, flour, sugar and tobacco from merchants. In Stevensville one merchant wouldn't sell to the Indians, but other shop owners profited more from his refusal. They used money for their transactions. The hostiles crossed Lolo Creek and ventured up a grade onto the Weippe Prairie, where there was water and grass. Some braves returned to Kamiah following Major Mason for several days as he pushed toward Missoula.

Joseph's Indian cavalry were extremely adept at stealing horses and combat. The braves began rounding up horses from Joseph's strays and stole ponies from peaceful Indians in the valley until they had rounded up a herd numbering 700 horses. These braves burned homes in Kamiah and stole livestock.

Howard assigned Major John Green and complement from Fort Boise to guard the Camas Prairie. He ordered more troops from Georgia and Washington Territory. Howard's personal command consisted of Captain Miller's 21st Infantry. Four companies were headed by Captain Evan Miles and four companies under Major Sanford.

He rested at Kamiah before continuing in pursuit of the hostiles. Howard had left half of his troops there, taking the remainder to pursue Joseph. The ascent above Kamiah with wagons and heavy guns was rugged with slippery trails, undergrowth, rocks and fallen timber. It was a 16 mile trek to Weippe Prairie.

Believing that they had won the fight, the soldiers began to burn the lodges but White Bird's warriors drove Gibbons back. Joseph engineered breaking camp and loading the pack-horses. His warriors captured Gibbon's canon and ammunition. They disabled the howitzer and left it lay. The braves started their own fire that raged toward the soldiers in the strong wind, but changed directions and died out. By evening 29 soldiers were dead and 40 injured, including Gibbons.

As General Howard arrived, the Indians disappeared. Joseph had lost 12 at Big Hole, including women and children. It was said that two of his wives were among the dead. Looking Glasses' daughter was slain and some of the best warriors were killed, including Rainbow and Five Wounds. Ironically, two of the three that had first initiated the rebellion, Walailtits and Red Moccasin Tops, died there. After burying his dead, Joseph continued his flight. He rallied his braves on higher ground out of rifle range and gathered up a number of ponies that had scattered during the fray. The Indians departed Big Hole Basin. The hostiles crossed back into what is now Idaho and Lemhi Canyon. Chief White Bird held council with the Shoshonis. He attempted to petition them to ally with the Nez Perce against General Howard. Being traditional enemies of the Nez Perce, the Shoshonis refused the offer.

Howard received word that the hostiles were raiding ranches. They were leaving the carcasses of the cattle they had slaughtered as they lay. The Nez Perce surrounded a ranch at Horse Prairie Creek. The settlers put up a fight but eight men were massacred. Chief White Bird was blamed for the attack. A keg of whiskey was obtained by the braves, which may have accounted for their actions. Howard attempted to cut off the renegades, who headed for Yellowstone. He sent Lieutenant George Bacon and forty men to intercept them at Targhee Pass. Captains Calloway and Norton arrived from Virginia City to reinforce General Howard's column.

The Big Hole fight was on Looking Glass' watch and he lost face for maintaining lack of security. Leaning Elk assumed his duties. After the Battle of Big Hole the Nez Perce held council and decided to raid Howard's camp for horses at Camas Meadows on August 17th.

War-chief Joseph was a leader, military genius and warrior-chief. His strategy in war was unsurpassed. He outwitted army military leaders time after time. He was an orator and statesman, a friend to the whites until they started the Nez Perce War (Courtesy A.P.)

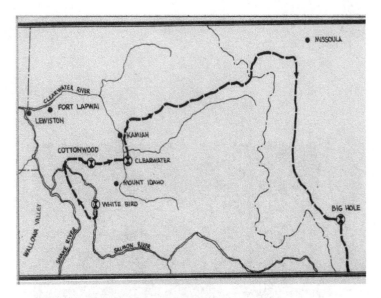

Route of War Chief Joseph's Retreat- Map of Joseph's Retreat in the Nez Perce War is from the initial battle at White Bird Creek to the Battle of Big Hole. (Courtesy I.H.S. L.)

Harper Weekly Magazine Cartoons were drawn by the magazine's artists in the autumn of 1877 depicting the Nez Perce War, battle by battle, as the nation watched with interest.
(Courtesy I.H.S.L.)

The general's men were tuckered so he pushed to reach Camas Meadows where they could camp and rest. With a heavy guard posted, the men had a false sense of security. Two Nez Perce had been seen milling around, but nothing was thought of it. In reality, they were Joseph's spies watching their every move. The camp of 150 soldiers bivouacked turning in for the night, thinking the Indians were a day's march away.

Joseph's scouts apprised him of Howard's position. 40 Nez Perce warriors stole in during the night, tricking the guards as they entered the camp. The sentry thought them to be soldiers. Joseph's warriors cut loose the mules, before being discovered. The Indians did not answer the sentry, so he discharged his weapon, awakening the camp. War-cries broke the silence, as the braves stampeded about 150 mules, by waving buffalo robes. The surprise caused pandemonium in the darkness. In the confusion, the men clamored to dress, find their guns and ammo. A bugler blew the call to attack.

The Indians drew fire as they rode out. Howard ordered his officers to recover the mules. Captains Carr, Jackson, and Norton took chase after the renegades to recapture the mules, which were far ahead of them. Carr led the advance, attacking the warriors with the mules. As Jackson and Norton joined Carr, the Indians initiated heavy resistance.

Cunning Joseph stationed snipers on all sides to surround the cavalry. The ensuing soldiers had to reign up, even though Norton was in trouble. Major Sanford called retreat. Lieutenant Benson stood for a moment and received a bullet through his buttocks. Carr recaptured the mules, but lost them again. The bugler blew retreat, as the other troops under heavy cross-fire withdrew. Joseph's double-flank movement succeeded. His warriors picked off many off the soldiers who were trying to reach their horses, some 500 yards away. Norton still engaged in fighting. It took Howard's full complement to rescue them. Seeing his advance, the Indians retreated. The army covered about 20 miles before returning to camp. Howard then pursued the hostiles, who now had a three day lead. Joseph continued along the Lo-Lo Trail, against the Rocky Mountains, toward Yellowstone.

W.T. Sherman, General of the Army, was in Yellowstone Park during a tour of the western forts. He was escorted by Lieutenant Colonel Gilbert and two troops of cavalry from Fort Benton, which was near Bozeman. General Sherman left the park, narrowly escaping a confrontation with the Nez Perce hostiles.

As the fugitives rode through Yellowstone, they encountered the Cowan party. They were tourists that had come to view the geysers from Helen. The Indians broke up their wagon and stole the camp equipment and supplies. Although the chiefs wanted to free the tourists, the unruly braves shot Cowan and left his body lying by the trail.

Another group of tourists in the Weikert party left Helena for Yellowstone Park. The renegades shot Mr. Weikert through his shoulder-blade while riding his horse. His mount stumbled on a log, throwing him.

Weikert still held his pistol and jumped to his feet, firing at the warriors. He remounted, still firing as the braves ran toward him. In the meantime, they pillaged the camp, stealing 14 horses, the blankets, tents and saddles. The red-skins proceeded to burn anything left over. The hostiles killed Mr. Kenk and stole a wad of bills from Mr. Stewart, but spared his life. Those of the party that escaped made it to safety. Some arrived at Mammoth Springs, nearby and two continued on 150 miles to Virginia City. Howard was never under manned. He always had scouts and keeping him informed and used the telegraph to track Joseph.

War Chief Joseph poses with the famous rifle he surrendered to General Howard. His days of retirement in Colville were saddened at the loss of family, warriors and fellow chiefs. The white man had taken everything he had known.

(Courtesy ISH.S.)

Nez Perce Chief Joseph's common name was Young Joseph or
Thunder-Traveling-over-the-Mountains. Chief Joseph became
known as a noble Redman to both Indian and white man. Joseph
was called the Patriotic Chief.   (Courtesy A.P.)

Military companies dispatched from around the country were constantly coming to join the fray. By keeping his numbers of fighting men up, Howard was never over powered.

Howard sent a currier to Sturgis, instructing him to travel at top speed along the Yellowstone River in an attempt to detain Joseph's Nez Perce, but the message arrived too late. In the interim, the Nez Perce killed two mountain men and a boy that Sturgis had deployed to reconnoiter. The trail of the renegades was discovered along the Stinking Water River. Looking Glass had ridden ahead to council with the Crow Indians, but they chose neutrality. A scout told Joseph that Sturgis was ahead and that the prairie was on fire. The Indians continued on toward Canada.

The Nez Perce at this time numbered 400 warriors strong. Joseph sent a group of his braves toward Hart Mountain, dragging bundles of brush behind their horses, hiding their tracks. Sturgis led the 7th cavalry after them, post haste. When Sturgis vacated, he left a clearing large enough for the Indians to travel through, as Joseph had planned. He eluded both Howard and Sturgis at Clark's Fork. Sturgis had been tricked. The officers met and decided that the lieutenant would still pursue the Indians. Colonial Sturgis intercepted him at Canyon Creek, by traveling west along the Yellowstone River and the Battle of Canyon Creek ensued.

Canyon Creek was a dry wash, surrounded by ten to twenty foot walls. The hostiles began firing from both sides of the canyon on September 13th but two of Sturgis' companies drove the Indians back.

They fought hard to regain ground and defend the women and children. Sturgis ordered Benteen to lead his cavalry around the hills and across the creek to try and cut off the horse herd. He then ordered Merrill's battalion to protect Benteen's left flank. As the cavalry rode out, the Indians anticipating their move, peppering them with bullets. The soldiers dismounted. Lt. Otis advanced on foot with his "Jackass Battery," The Nez Perce drove them back. Sturgis' plan backfired.

Captain French's Company M gave boisterous yells, as they rushed up the hillside in an effort to reach the Indians. Some were on horseback, others on foot. Seeing a group of warriors in a huddle, the soldiers fired directly on them, killing some. The Seventh advanced onto the valley floor and were met with a barrage of Indians' bullets. The sniper fire pinned them down. Joseph had held Sturgis. The soldiers made camp, being exhausted. During the night, Joseph's Nez Perce broke camp and continued their retreat. With the army's advantage of howitzers, 21 Nez Perce died, while the army lost 3, with 11 wounded.

The next day, Joseph's people entered "the land of the Crows." It wasn't the nirvana that Chief Looking Glass had hoped for. Instead, it was another fight. Their old enemies, the Crow Indians had been expecting them. A running battle began that stretched over 150 miles of hard fighting. The Nez Perce lost nearly 900 spent horses that day. The Crows continued fought them within 40 miles of the Musselshell River.

Nez Perce braves commandeered a stagecoach and burned the way station and buildings. The young bucks took turns driving and riding on and in the coach. The braves toyed with the stage until they became bored, when they destroyed it and burned the mail. The driver and the passengers escaped into the brush to be rescued by Howard.

The Indians had out distanced Sturgis and soldiers. They traveled along the Musselshell River, while Joseph made a wide sweep west around the Judith Mountains. On September 23th, they reached the freight depot on Cow Island.

The Indians crossed the Missouri River and attacked the garrison. It was sheltered by a small earthwork structure, guarded by Sergeant William Mulchert, twelve soldiers of the Seventh Cavalry and four citizens, who defended over 50 tons of supplies (both government and private). The goods had been recently unloaded from the Steamship Benton onto the bank of the river. The steamer had departed down the Missouri a short time before the Nez Perce raid. At one time, Joseph offered to surrender for 200 bags of sugar; he was asked to surrender anyway, but the Indians stole the sugar. The hostiles helped themselves to all of the supplies that they wanted and burned the remainder. The "Skirmish at Cow Island" lasted 18 hours, two volunteers were wounded.

Major Ilges and 36 volunteers left Fort Benton for Cow Island. On September 25th, Ilges began tracking the hostiles up Cow Creek Canyon. Lieutenant Hardin brought soldiers down river by boat. After ten miles a scout located the Indian encampment. The insurgents had surrounded a wagon-train near Judith Basin. As the soldiers arrived, the Indians set fire to the wagons as seven emigrants fled into the hills. The Nez Perce rode down the canyon for about one half mile, attacking the troops. As they left, the warriors broke off into small groups and disappeared.

The major and his men had taken cover. From the high ground the Indians initiated gunfire. The fracas started about noon and for two hours they fought. The Indians were terribly accurate with their rifles, without showing themselves. They ceased firing from the front. Major Ilges suspected a rear offensive and retreated to Cow Island. Snipers held them

LAWYER.

Lawyer Drawing (1889) - Lawyer was a Nez Perce Sub-chief under Chief Joseph, earning his rank in battle. Lawyer was among other Nez Perce chiefs to sign the treaty of 1868 reducing the size of their reservation. Lawyer stayed on the reservation during the Nez Perce War and retreat to Canada.

(Courtesy I. H. S. L.)

down until the main body of Nez Perce escaped. One citizen and a horse had been killed, while two Indians were injured. Joseph anticipated no opposition through the buffalo country. Miles got the idea to shell the bluff with big guns in order to signal the steamship to return. The Benton and crew returned to Cow Island Crossing.

The end of September, 1877 the Nez Perce camped along the Milk River aided with ample drinking water and firewood. The tribe had ample time to rest. Horses could graze and gain back the weight they had lost from constantly being on the move or in battle. They had plenty of antelope, buffalo, and deer to provide their meat supply and winter robes. The Indians could relax with Howard far behind them. They built up their winter stores on the Milk River, rested and tended their wounds.

They continued on, reaching the vicinity of the Bear Paw Mountains, 1300 miles from Wallowa Valley and just 40 miles from the Canadian border. Rain mixed with snow as the tribe faced the task of the last leg of their journey. Joseph and his twelve year old daughter readied their horses and adjusted the loads, anticipating their quest.

Out of nowhere, from the south rode a line of cavalrymen charging the camp. Fifty or sixty braves guarded the horses. Miles had the advantage, with 600 cavalrymen, infantry, and his Cheyenne Indian scouts. His complement was equipped with a breech-loading Hotchkiss gun and a twelve pound Napoleon cannon. Miles used a double line of the 2nd and 7th Cavalry in an attempt to divide and conquer in a single charge. Joseph and his daughter were cut off from the camp. He gave her a rope and told her to tether the horses, before joining the others that were isolated. Joseph broke and ran through the melee. Reaching his lodge, his wife handed Joseph his rifle and said, "go and fight."

159

Miles' column caught Joseph, splitting his ranks. Joseph's brother, Ollokut was killed. Joseph rushed to his family and though greatly outnumbered, the Nez Perce pushed the soldiers back. Miles held his ground. The Cavalry stampeded the Indians' horses. Miles lost 26 men and 40 were wounded. Joseph lost 18 men and 3 women. He stated that if they had wanted to leave the women, children and injured; they could have left the country.

Chief Joseph finally sent Yellow Bull to talk with General Miles, who demanded surrender, assuring safe passage. Yellow Bull wondered if Miles was sincere. Some Cheyenne scouts spoke with Joseph and told him that they believed Miles truly wanted peace. Joseph met with Miles, with no answer. On the fifth day of talks on October 5, 1877, War Chief Joseph surrendered, giving up his rifle. He uttered those famous words, "Here me my chiefs, I am tired. My heart is sick and sad. From where the sun now stands, I will fight no more forever." His flight for freedom to King George's land had failed. The long journey was over.

At the time, General Miles had promised if Joseph surrendered, the Nez Perce could go back home. General Miles and his troops escorted Joseph and his people to Tongue River, and they were taken to Bismark, against Miles wishes. They were ordered to Leavenworth and were forced to live by a river that was unclean. They bathed, drink and cooked from that river, causing many deaths. From Leavenworth, they were shipped by rail to Baxter, in Kansas Territory. Three died in the box-cars. There was no medical assistance and 70 Nez Perce died of exposure. Joseph told officials of Miles promise to return to Wallowa, but was stated that it was impossible. He and 150 of his tribe were exiled for a time in Indian Territory in Oklahoma and lastly shipped by rail to

Young Chief Joseph loved his country. His father had told him never to give up the land that held his peoples' bones. When he became chief, Joseph endeavored to keep the promise to Old Joseph. He fought a good fight, but lost. A.P.)

Joseph in the Bear Paw Mountains harbored much sadness in his defeat. Proud, War-chief Joseph surrendered to save his people's lives and lost his freedom, homeland and thousands of horses. (Courtesy Frank Wasson)

Princess Sarah Winnemucca was born to a chief in western Nevada. Sarah was a champion of her people and a crusader during the Bannock War. In later years she became an orator and author working for the cause of her Paiutes. She was made chief of the Northern Paiutes, for saving her people.

(Courtesy of the Nevada Historical Society)

Chief Winnemucca II- Winnemucca in the Paiute language meant "One Moccasin." The chief's father was Truckee or Chief Winnemucca. Chief Winnemucca II was a proponent of the Paiute War because of an evil Indian agent who stole the Paiute's rations, causing the Indians to go hungry.

(Courtesy of the Nevada Historical Society)

the Colville Reservation, in eastern Washington Territory. Joseph never saw his Wallowa Valley again. Broken hearted, Joseph died before his teepee fire September 21, 1904.

Because of broken treaties, Buffalo Horn prepared for war, while Chief Tendoy chose peace. He and his group rode to the Lemhi River Reservation. Buffalo Horn's band of 200 Bannocks went on the warpath attacking cattlemen on the Camas Prairie, killing two. While a third man hid in the brush, another fled on horseback to spread the word of attack to Fort Boise, contacting Captain Bernard.

The marauders plundered wagons near King Hill, stealing arms, and fled across the Snake River using the ferry. Reaching the other side, they cut it loose. The Bannocks killed some settlers at the mouth of the Bruneau River. Captain Egan along with 46 Bannocks and Weiser Indians joined Buffalo Horn. His band increased to 300.

Bernard's column pursued Buffalo Horn over the divide to the headwaters of the Owyhee River. Some 20 volunteers, stationed at Silver City, reached the hostiles first and engaged them, meeting heavy fire. They retreated in a running battle; Chief Buffalo Horn was supposedly killed in the siege. Egan replaced Buffalo Horn and their numbers grew to 800, as others joined them, outnumbering Bernard and his men, three to one. It was rumored that Buffalo Horn lived and escaped to Wyoming.

Howard left Fort Walla-Walla for Boise June 9, 1878 and by June 18th, had raised 900 troops, six officers and artillery to handle the outbreak. Captain Bernard and several other excellent officers joined General Howard's columns to engage Egan's band.

There is a folk story about a chief seen by trappers along the Humboldt River, wearing only one moccasin. Once, he came into town wearing little of nothing. Old Chief Winnemucca was given an army uniform and hat, which he liked and wore. In the Paiute tongue, winni, is one and mucca means moccasin. The people called him "One Moccasin."

Winnemucca or During the Bannock War the hostiles took Chief Winnemucca II and the Malheur Paiutes at the reservation captive, taking their blankets, horses and weapons. When Sarah Winnemucca learned of her father's plight, she rode to Sheep Camp. She arrived desperate to find her father. Sarah met with Army General Howard who gave her a letter of safe passage. Picking up the Bannock's tracks, Sarah rode after them.

From a high overlook Sarah surveyed the Bannock camp of several hundred teepees. At nightfall she descended the slope, concealed under a blanket and war-paint. Sarah entered the chief's tent. During the night, she ushered her father out of camp and was joined by her brother, his wife and two cousins, who had come to help. They held the horses and aided in their escape to Sheep Camp. From there, the army escorted Sarah, her father and family to Fort McDermott and safety. Sarah and her sister-in-law later worked for the army as couriers.

The marauders meantime rode toward the John Day River, in Oregon Territory, killing ranchers and stealing livestock and proceeded along the Grand River into the Blue Mountains. The hostiles were now made up of Malheur, Paiute, Shoshoni, Umatilla, and Weiser Indians.

The savages continued their rampage, killing and pillaging; on the move, they covered hundreds of miles. The rebels fought, whenever the Cavalry overtook them, who purposely kept the renegades on the run.

Captain Egan crossed the Columbia River, offering the Umatilla Indians 2,000 horses to join them in battle. When they refused, the rebels opened fire on them. This time, the Umatilla offered to join them.

165

Chief Joseph, grown older now, relaxes in his teepee. After the siege, Joseph was moved around from reservation to reservation. He was in Oklahoma Indian Territory. Finally, Joseph and other members of his tribe were put on boxcars and shipped to the reservation in Colville, Washington Territory.

(Courtesy I.H.S.L.)

Immediately, the Umatilla began firing, killing Captain Egan. The rebels fled and rode into Montana, where Captain Miles, his troops and Indian Scouts pulled an early morning raid ending the Bannock War.

In (1872) Smohalla, a Nez Perce prophet proclaimed that Indians would rise up from the dead and drive the white-eyes out of the land, initiating the Dreamer's Religion.

Wavoca, a Paiute holy man in Nevada, whom the whites called Jack Wilson, had a vision of immortal warriors in Ghost shirts dancing in a circle, invincible to white man's bullets, in "The Ghost Shirt Religion". The frenzy spread, influencing hundreds of Indians to rally and fight the white man with hope of redemption. Brule Sioux Chief Crow Dog was active in the Ghost Shirt Dance Movement and is known for killing Brule Sioux Chief Spotted Tail.

It was 1879 when the Sheep-eater Shoshoni were accused of stealing horses from settlers. Two prospectors were killed, near Cascade and five Chinese were killed, near Loon, Creek. Colonel Bernard and his Company G, 1st Cavalry left Boise Barracks (Fort Boise,) riding hard north, to intercept the warring Sheep-eaters. Those who chose war found themselves engaged with the Cavalry and their fight was short lived.

Buffalo Bill Cody started the first Rodeo and Wild West Show. Buffalo Bill's female sharpshooter heroine, Annie Oakley, was a big draw. His real live Indians and cowboys and his great promotion put the legendary west into perspective in American hearts and minds.

Sitting Bull made just one tour with William Fredrick Cody's Wild West Show in 1885. Chiefs American Horse, Red Cloud and Spotted Tail had worked for Buffalo Bill in his Wild West Show also.

167

Cody recreated Custer's Last Stand with soldiers and Indians fighting. In addition, Buffalo Bill had live bears and buffalo to add to the excitement.

Word traveled fast about the Ghost Dance in Nevada to Fort Hall and into the Plains, reaching the Sioux. (1890) Young Sioux braves did the Ghost Dance in their sacred shirts one night, giving war-whoops, shooting off rifles and dancing around a huge bonfire late in the night at Wounded Knee.

It frightened nearby settlers. The U.S. Cavalry was called in the next day. Chief Sitting Bull was pulled from his sleeping robes and shot to death Sitting Bull's death was the passing of an era.

Many Plains Tribes had surrendered to General Miles in his 1876-77 Campaign. At Pine Ridge Sitting Bull, with the Brule and Oglala Sioux had resisted.

After the Ghost Dance in 1890, 300 Sioux Indian Ghost dancers of all ages were killed at Wounded Knee, South Dakota ending in massacre by the U.S. Seventh Cavalry with lots of manpower and cannons. Buffalo Soldiers accompanied them. Sioux Chief Big Foot surrendered. The Medicine Man's dream became a nightmare.

Buffalo Bill Cody and Sitting
Bull-Sitting Bull did one world-tour
with Buffalo Bill's Wild West Show
in 1885. Buffalo Bill used real cowboys
and Indians to portray the "Old West,"
and a cowgirl trick-shot, named
Annie Oakley.   (Courtesy of A. P.)

Buffalo Bill Cody's first Wild West
Show and rodeo were held in North
Platte, Nebraska during a July 4th
Celebration and its premiere was in
Columbus, Nebraska. Bill had real
cowboys and wild Indian chiefs in
his show.   (Courtesy of A. P.)

Disappearing American Indian
(Courtesy of Azusa Publishing Company)

Conclusion

The Shoshone-Bannock Fort Hall Indian Reservation is located in southeastern Idaho, eight miles north of Pocatello. The reservation was established in Fort Hall by the Fort Bridger Treaty of 1868. The Shoshoni Indians at Fort Hall were given 1.8 million acres, initially by the Great White Father (President of the United States) and has been reduced to 544,000 acres. The government gave every adult Indian 160 acres and 80 acres to each child. A seven member council was established in 1936, called the Fort Hall Business Council, with a law and order code. 3500 Indians actively reside at Fort Hall, with 5,000 actual members. The tribe has a tribal credit bureau, employment agency and recreation organization.

Duck Valley Indian Reservation was first established in 1877 and enlarged in 1886. The Shoshone-Paiute Reservation lies on the Idaho-Nevada border, half in each state (in Owyhee County, Idaho and Elko County, Nevada). The Shoshone-Paiute Tribes maintain 289,820 acres of land. 1265 Native Americans were living on the Duck Valley Indian Reservation in year, 2,000. Agriculture is the main income resource. 87,000 acres are farmed and cattle and horses are grazed there. Sheep Creek and Mountain View Reservoirs provide fishing on the reservation. A third reservoir, the Billie Shaw is being dug. Shore birds and waterfowl flock to the wetland areas in numbers. The public can camp, bird watch, fish or just relax and enjoy the recreation area.

The Nez Perce Indian Reservation is in the Columbia River Plateau, located in Idaho, Oregon and Washington, including the Clearwater, Salmon and Snake Rivers. The population for the reservation was 17,959 tribes-people in 2,000. The Nez Perce Tribe has an Appaloosa horse breeding program. Fishers in the tribe are active in tribal fisheries on the Columbia River, between Bonneville and McNairy Dams. They also fish for Chinook salmon and steelhead during the spring and summer runs. The Nez Perce Tribe operates a fish hatchery on the Clearwater River and other hatcheries. The largest town on the reservation is Orofino, in northeastern Idaho.

There are eight Sioux Indian Reservations in South Dakota. The Great Sioux Nation was established in 1868. The Rosebud Sioux Reservation was established, then. The eight Sioux Reservations are as follows: the Cheyenne River Sioux, Crow Creek Sioux, Flandreau-Santee Sioux, Lower Brule Sioux, Pine Ridge Sioux, Rosebud Sioux, Sisseton-Wahpeton Sioux and the Yankton Sioux.

171

INDEX

A

Aboriginal peoples, 11
American Fur Trade, 47
Archeologist, Tom Green, 87
Astor Expedition, 32
atlatl, 21

B

Bannock, 13
Bannock Indians, 13
Battle of the Clearwater, 115
Bear River Shoshoni, 13
Black Hills, 94
Blackfoot, 23, 37
Blue Mountains, 41
Boise City, 11
Boise River, 32
Bruneau River Shoshoni, 80
Bruneau River Shoshonis, 13
Buffalo Horn, 111, 129
Buffalo hunters, 11
Buffalo jump, 17

C

Camas Meadows, 121
Camas Prairie, 129
Camp Boise River, 77
Camp River Boise, 11
Canoe Camp Lewis and Clark, 28
Captain Bernard, 129
Captain Bonneville, 55
Captain Egan, 131

Captain Gray Discovered the Columbia River, 37
Captain Miles, 116
Captain Nathaniel J. Wyeth, 41
Captain Rawn, 117
Captain Whipple, 114
Cayuse Indian, 43
Chief Eagle-Eye, 94
Chief Joseph, 103
Chief Looking Glass, 103, 111
Chief Red Cloud Sioux, 94
Chief Washakie, 53
Chief White Bird, 120
Christopher Columbus, 47
Christopher Houston Carson, 55
Chuck wagons, 61
Comanche Indians, 21
Conestoga, 59
Conquistadors Spanish, 11
Continental Divide, 11
Cop-cop-pa-ala, 21
Cottonwood, 111
Coyote, 19
Crazy Horse Sioux chieftan, 94
Crow country, 23
Crow Indian scouts, 97

D

David Thompson, 67
Donald McKenzie, 37
Dr. John McLoughlin Fort Vancouver, 39
Duck Valley Indian Reservation, 135

E

Eagle, Idaho, 32
Europeans, 11

F

Fort Astoria, 34
Fort Benton, 124
Fort Boise, 11, 69
Fort Bridger, 53
Fort Bridger Treaty of 1868, 135
Fort Colt Killed Camp Lewis and Clark, 27
Fort Hall, 69, 80
Fort Hall Shoshoni, 13
Fort Kearney, 75
Fort Laramie, 67
Fort Snake, 71
Fort Vancouver, 67
Fur Trade Era, 49

G

Gaming, 21
General George Crook, 85
General Gibbon, 120
General Howard, 94, 111, 129
General Sturgis, 122
George Armstrong Custer Lt. Colonel, 97
George Grimes, 91
Ghost Dance, 132
Glenn's Ferry, 61

172

H

Hear me my chiefs, 125
Hell's Canyon., 99
Henry Hudson, 35
Henry Spalding, 41
Hudson's Bay
    Company
    British, 11

I

Indian Wars, 7, 11, 67, 69, 73, 77, 83, 84, 85, 91
In-mut-too-yah-lat-lat or Joseph Thunder Rolling over the Mountains, 102
Iron Horse, 65

J

Jedediah Strong S, 55
Jim Bridger, 53
John C. Fremont, 71
John McLoughlin, 11
Johnithon Keeney, 75

K

King Charles, 35

L

land of the Crows, 124
Lapwai, 43, 103
Le Clerc, 32
Lemhi Shoshoni, 19
Lewis and Clark, 27
Little Big Horn., 108
Long Camp

Lewis and Clark, 30
longhouse, 19
Louisiana Purchase, 27

M

Major Lugenbeel, 75, 77
Manuel Lisa party, 30
Marie Dorion, 30

N

Nampa
    Bigfoot, 63
Nez Perce, 99
Nez Perce Indian Reservation, 135
Norseman, 11
Northern Paiute, 13
Northwest Company, 37
Northwest Territory, 37

O

Ollokut, 111
Oregon Territory, 35
Oregon Trail, 59
Owyhee Desert, 73

P

Pacific Fur Company, 67
Palouse Indians, 91
Peace Valley, 17
Peter Skene Ogden, 37
Peter Stuyvesant, 51
Pierre Dorion Jr, 30
Pierre Dorion, Sr., 34
Pinkney Lugenbeel Major, 11
pony bead, 49

Prairie Schooner, 59
President Abraham Lincoln, 11
President Thomas Jefferson, 27

R

rabbit drives, 15
Rev. Whitman, 41
Rocky Mountains, 73
Rosebud Sioux village, 97

S

Sacajawea, 9, 25, 27, 28, 30, 33, 34, 75
Salmon Festival, 17
Salmon River Shoshonis, 13
Sarah Winnemucca, 129
Scalp Dance, 13
scalps, 23
Sheep Camp, 129
Sheep-Eater Shoshoni, 13
Shoshone-Bannock Fort Hall, 135
Sitting Bull
    Medicine man & Chief, 94
Smohalla
    Nez Perce Prophet, 131
Snake Indians, 13
Snake River, 17
Snake River Plain, 71
Snake River Plains, 17
soddie, 78
Starr Wilkinson, 63

T

teepee, 19
Texas Rangers, 94

Thomas McKay, 69
Toohulhutsote, 115
Trade Fair, 17

U

U.S. Seventh Cavalry,
133

W

Walking Shoshoni, 17
Wallowa, 103
Ward massacre, 63
Wavoka
    Paiute Shaman, 25
Weippe Prairie, 116
Weiser River
    Shoshonis, 13
Western Shoshoni, 13
White Bird Canyon,
    106
Whitman's Mission,
    43
William Fredrick Cody
    Buffalo Bill, 131
William Thomas
    Sherman
    General over the
        Army, 121
Wounded Knee
    South Dakota, 132

Y

Yellow Bull, 125
Yellowstone Park, 121

Bibliography

Addison, Helen and McGrath, Dan L., War Chief Joseph, Lincoln, Nebraska, Third Bison Book Printing, 1967.

Barbour, Barton H., Fort Union and the Upper Mississippi Fur Trade, Norman, University of Oklahoma Press, 2001.

Beal, Merrill D., "I Will Fight No More Forever," New York, Ballantine Books, 1971.

Bird, Laurie Annie, Old Fort Boise, Caldwell, Idaho, Caxton Printers, Ltd., 1971.

Brown, Dee, Bury My Heart At Wounded Knee, New York, Bantam, 1972.

Bryce, George, The Remarkable History of the Hudson's Bay Company, London, Sampson, Marston and Company Ltd., 1900.

Dary, David, The Oregon Trail, an American Saga, New York, Oxford University Press, 2004.

Derig, Betty, Roadside History of Idaho, Missoula, Mt., Mountain Press Publishing Company,1996.

Hailey, John, History of Idaho, Boise, Syms-York, 1910.

Kloss, Doris, Sarah Winnemucca, Minneapolis, Dillon Press, 1986.

Lowell, Helen & Peterson, Lucile, Our First One Hundred Years, Caldwell, Idaho, Caxton Printers, Ltd., 1999.

Members of the Potomac Corral, Great Western Indian Fights, Lincoln, Nebraska, Bison Books, 1966.

Newman, Peter C., Company of Adventurers, New York, Viking Press, 1985.

O'Neal, Bill, Best of the West, Lincolnwood, Illinois, Publications International, Ltd., 2006.

Salisbury, Albert & Jane, Lewis & Clark, the Journey West, New York, Promontory Press, 1990.

Shannon, Donald H., The Boise Massacre on the Oregon Trail, Caldwell, Idaho, Snake River Publishers, 2004.

Steward, Julian H., Plateau Aboriginal Sociopolitical Groups, Salt Lake, University of Utah Press, 1970.

Utley, Robert M., Encyclopedia of the American West, New York, Random House, 1997.

Welsh, James & Stekler, Paul, Killing Custer, New York, Norton and Company, 1994.

Wilson, Amy, Comparative Analysis of Bead Assemblages from the Fur Trade Posts Fort Colville and Fort Vancouver, /Thesis (M.S.)-University of Idaho, 1996.

Citing Electronic Publications

<http:// en.wikipedia.org/wiki/Hudson's_Bay_Company>

<http://en.wikipedia.org/wiki/Nez_Perce>

<http:tripcheck.com/poses/SBhellcanyon.asp>

<http:www.bigfootforums.com/lofiversion/index.php/tii5.68.html>

<http:www.clarkontheyellowstone.org/sig_event.html>

<http:www.en.wikipedia.org/wiki/Fort_Boise>

<http:www.en.wikipedia.org/wiki/Fort_Vancouver>

<http:www.enwikipedia.org/wiki/Jim_Bridger>

<http:www.enwikipedia.org/wiki/Lewis_and_Clark_Expedition>

<http:www.enwikipedia.org/wiki/Washakie>

<http:www.geocities.com/naforts/id.html>

<http:www.home.att.net/~mman/DoriansWife.htm>

<http:www.kstrom.net/isk/maps/Dakotas/sd.html>

<http:www.legendsofAmerica.com/id-forthall.html>

<http:www.mountaintrappers.org/history/hudsons.htm>

<http:www.nps.gov/archive/fola/Laramie.htm>

<http:www.primitiveways.com/tule_ethnobotany.html>

<http:www.shoshonebannocktribes.com>

<http:www.thefurtrapper.com/historical_landmarks.htm>

<http:www.washingtonwars.net/Ward%20Massacre.htm>

<http:www.xroads.virginia.edu/HNS/BuffaloBill/home.html>

The Author explores inside of a 19th Century stone house in southeastern Oregon.

About the Author

Born in Lexington, Nebraska, Robb Bolen is part Indian, and has a B.A. degree in Archeology. The author's ancestors erected Fort Bolin near Cross Creek, Pennsylvania for protection from Indian attacks (1777). Four Bolen's fought under George Washington, in the Revolutionary War. A female ancestor was kidnapped by Shawnee Indians and held captive for one year before she was being rescued. Two Bolen's were killed in Kentucky by Shawnees, who were allied to the British. Great grand-dad Gilbert Bolen fought in the Civil War with the Ohio 4th Cavalry under General Sherman. (1866) Gilbert came west with his wife and six kids in a Conestoga wagon. Robb's grand-dad, Denver Colorado Bolen, knew "Buffalo Bill Cody," as a young man in western Nebraska. The author now resides in Nampa, Id outside of Boise.

PHOTOGRAPHS
COURTESY OF
AZUSA Publishing, LLC
3575 S. Fox Street
Englewood, CO 80110

Email: azusa@azusapublishing.com
Phone Toll-free: 888-783-0077
Phone/Fax: 303-783-0073

Email: azusa@azusapublishing.com
**Mailing address: P.O. Box 2526, Englewood,
CO 80150**

CPSIA information can be obtained
at www.ICGtesting.com
Printed in the USA
LVHW041828200819
628309LV00013B/862/P

9 780615 231464